MARBLES BEYOND GLASS

Stanley A. Block

Schiffer Publishing Ltd®

4880 Lower Valley Road, Atglen, PA 19310 USA

Dedication

This book is dedicated to all of the collectors, contemporary artists, and rock hounds who have contributed to its completion, and to the continuing growth of the hobby of marbles.

Library of Congress Control Number: 2005934198

Cover and book Designed by Bruce Waters
Type set in Franklin Gothic TC HV BT/Garamond

ISBN: 0-7643-2363-6
Printed in China

Published by Schiffer Publishing Ltd.
4880 Lower Valley Road
Atglen, PA 19310
Phone: (610) 593-1777; Fax: (610) 593-2002
E-mail: Info@schifferbooks.com

For the largest selection of fine reference books on this and related subjects, please visit our web site at
www.schifferbooks.com
We are always looking for people to write books on new and related subjects. If you have an idea for a book please contact us at the above address.

This book may be purchased from the publisher.
Include $3.95 for shipping.
Please try your bookstore first.
You may write for a free catalog.

In Europe, Schiffer books are distributed by
Bushwood Books
6 Marksbury Ave.
Kew Gardens
Surrey TW9 4JF England
Phone: 44 (0) 20 8392-8585; Fax: 44 (0) 20 8392-9876
E-mail: info@bushwoodbooks.co.uk
Free postage in the U.K., Europe; air mail at cost.

Contents

Acknowledgments

I would like to thank and acknowledge all who have aided in the completion of this book and the society projects. The collections, artists, friends, and family who have aided us in our efforts have certainly contributed immensely to the completion of this project. It is the culmination of twelve years of photography of marbles and related items from all over the country. A special thanks to the collectors who have brought examples to the various shows we attended, so that we could photograph them.

A very special thanks to Peter Schiffer and his professional staff for their help and expertise in getting this work published and into the hands of the public. Without their efforts this book would not have been published.

Thank You All

— Stanley Block
Chairman

Introduction

Welcome to the wonderful world of marbles. This book is a photographic manual and compilation of currently known information about marbles made with materials other than glass. It is another part of our work in progress, to help those interested in the hobby of marbles to learn to recognize the various types that exist as well as their differences, collectability, and value.

Our goal here is to cover all of the types of marbles made of materials other than glass. Glass marbles are covered in detail in our other books. See the listing on the inside back of the dust cover.

Each of the sections of this volume has a multitude of photographs of examples taken by photographers during the past twelve years from collections all over North America. Our thanks go out to all of the collectors who have allowed us to photograph their marbles. Photographs that do not have a collector acknowledgement in the caption come from either the author's collection or the collection of the Marble Collector's Society of America.

Marbles made of stone, clay, and pottery have been found in archaeological digs going back to ancient Egyptian tombs. The earliest known marbles were stream tumbled and rounded stone marbles. These were followed by clay, pottery, and early mosaic glass varieties. Obviously, marbles of one type or another have been popular children's toys from the time the first rounded stone was found. During the 1400s, the Church of England declared Good Friday as Marbles Day — supposedly to keep the children occupied, so as not to be rowdy during the day's church services.

The toy continued to grow in popularity and many variations of marble games came into being. The increase in popularity spawned a whole industry and the use of a variety of types and materials. During the 1800s and early 1900s, marbles were made of minerals and stone, clays, pottery, crockery, porcelain, china, and glass. Among the most highly prized marbles were banded agates that were hand cut, milled, and polished. The best of these were produced as a cottage industry in Idar-Oberstein, Germany. Another popular type was the hand-painted china. However, the majority of demand came for the less costly clays, crockeries, and pottery types.

As times changed and technology improved, marbles were made from other materials such as plastics, metals, cements, and fiber optics. Improvements in machines led to increased demand for, and usage of, all sorts of minerals in marble making, bowls, and spheres. This growth paralled the growth in glass marbles, from handmade to machine-made types.

Included within each section of this book is a price guide. Four factors determine the value of a marble. They are type, size, condition, and eye appeal. For more comprehensive pricing, we recommend consulting the most recent edition of The Marbles Collectors Society price guide, *Marbles: Identification and Price Guide* by Robert Block (Schiffer Publishing).

Following the various sections of this book are sources to help the potential new collector or the advanced collector find sources of information. There are many marble shows held each year in various parts of the country. A calendar of these shows is included. It is our recommendation that you try to get to at least one show or meet, as you will learn more from attending one show by handling marbles and talking to other collectors than you will learn from the books. Books are great reference items, but there is nothing better than handling and viewing marbles in person. Be sure to check with the contact person shown on the listing to verify the dates, time, and place and to answer any other questions.

Also included at the back of the book are sources of information and a listing of marble clubs.

Marble Collectors Society of America

The Marble Collectors Society of America was founded in 1975 as a non-profit organization established for charitable, scientific, literary, and educational purposes. The Society's objectives are to gather and disseminate information and perform services to further the hobby of marbles, marble collecting, and the preservation of the history of marbles and marble making.

Society projects include the quarterly newsletter, *Marble Mania*, color marble photographic plates, a videotape series, and contributor's listings. In addition, we are in the process of ongoing research, and the development of a collection of marbles for the Society library.

Other major accomplishments of the Society to date are the uninterrupted issuance of its quarterly newsletter, *Marble Mania*; various surveys; photographing and publishing color sheets; gathering and placing collections in museums (The Smithsonian, The Corning Museum of Glass, and the Wheaton Village Museum); publication of price guides, with periodic updates; work toward establishing a library of articles and marble related materials; preparation of slide presentations; preparation and publication of contributor listings; research and issuance of articles concerning marble factories and contemporary marble makers; publication of Mark Randall's booklet, *Marbles as Historical Artifacts*; preparation of videotapes on marbles, including the first two-hour videotape on collecting marbles; classification and appraisal services; as well as the books *Marble Mania*, and Robert Block's *Marbles: Identification and Price Guide*. In addition to the above, the Society is working on additional tabletop books covering all facets of the hobby of marbles. These books will expand on the book *Marble Mania* that was published in 1998.

Each book will be a photographic manual, covering a specific section of the hobby, and each book is planned to contain over 500 photographs. The first of these expanded books, *Contemporary Marbles and Related Art Glass*, by Mark Block, was published in January 2001. It contains over 800 photographs, representing well over 100 glass artisans.

The next book published, *Sulphide Marbles*, was authored by Stanley Block and M. Edwin Payne, with an Introduction by Robert Block, and was published in May 2001. The hardcover book, *Sulphide Marbles*, contains over 600 photographs and is the first of three books covering antique handmade glass marbles. The series was continued with *Antique Glass Swirl Marbles* by Stanley Block, published in 2001, and *Antique End of Day Marbles* by Stanley Block, published in 2003.

The second book, *Antique Glass Swirl Marbles* by Stanley Block, published in October 2001, is another hardcover book detailing all of the swirl types with over 850 photographs and text.

The third and final book on the subject of antique handmade glass marbles covers End-of-Day and other handmade glass marbles not covered in the previous two books by the MCSA. Types contained in Section II of this book include, Clearies, Lightning Strike, Mica, Mosaic, Opaque, Paperweight, Patch, and Slag marbles. It was published in April 2002 and contains 190 pages and over 900 illustrations.

The next book issued was published in October 2003 and is the first in a series of books covering "machine-made marbles." Titled *Collecting Early Machine-Made Marbles: The M.F. Christensen & Son Company and Christensen Agate Company* by Robert S. Block, the book contains 160 pages and over 660 illustrations. Each of the books in the machine-made series will cover company histories, patents, marbles, and marble related items produced, as well as a price guide.

The current volume covers the balance of marble types. It includes over 900 illustrations on 160 pages, as well as price guides for each section.

Section I: Mineral and Stone

Stream tumbled, rounded stone marbles are the first known marbles that were used as children's toys. Earliest examples were rough and not totally round. Over generations, this popular type has grown and expanded to the point where almost every mineral can be made into a marble.

With the evolution of sphere making machines and the growth and popularity of the hobby of marbles, the following list of known stone and mineral marbles has grown to over 100. The listing will obviously continue to expand. Ten years ago a similar listing contained twenty-one examples. Included in this section are photos of at least forty-five of the mineral and stone marbles that are on the following listing.

Agate marbles, especially dyed banded agates, are still one of the most sought after types. Those that were cut, milled, and polished during the late 1800s and early 1900s in Idar Oberstein, Germany, are the most desirable. The colors and banding in those earlier agates are much brighter and more uniform compared to those that have more recently been made.

One way to distinguish the earlier examples from the newer ones is to hold the marble under a bright light and turn it slowly. You can usually see a facet or group of facets to show the marble was hand-cut before milling and polishing. In any case, the agate itself is thousands of years old.

The variety of materials that can be fashioned into marbles and spheres is almost limitless since there can be many combinations of two or more minerals in the same piece of material used.

Known Mineral Marbles

*Agate - Banded
*Agate - Carnelian
*Agate - Lace
*Agate - Picture
Amazonite
Amber
*Amethyst
Ametrine
Ammonite
*Angelite
Anhydrite
Apatite
Aquamarine
*Aragonite
Astrophillite
*Aventurine
Azurite
*Bloodstone
Brazilianite
Bustamite
Calcite
Chalcopyrite
Charoite
*Chert
Chirstalite
*Chrysocolla
Chrysoprase
Citrine
Copper
Coral
Damoltierite
Eudialite
*Fluorite
Fuschite
Galena
Garnet
*Goldstone
*Granite
Hematite
Holmquisite
*Howlite
Illmenite
*Jade
*Jasper
Jet
Labradorite
*Lapis Lazuli
Lazurite
*Leopardskin
Limestone
Lodolite
Magnesite
*Malachite
Marble
Mariposite
Meteorite
Moldavite
Mookaite
Moonstone
Morganite
*Obicular
*Obsidian
Olivine
*Onyx
*Opal
Opalite
Pectolite
*Petrified Palm
Pietersite
*Porphry
Prehenite
Pyrite
*Quartz - Optical
*Quartz - Rose
*Quartz - Rutilated
*Quartz - Smoky
*Rhodenite
*Rhodochrosite
Richtorite
*Ruby
*Sapphire
Sardonyx
Scorzalite
Selenite

Septarian
Seraphenite
*Serpentine
Sphalerite
*Sodalite
*Stromatolite
Sugulite
Sunstone
Thulite
*Tiger Iron
*Tigereye - Blue
*Tigereye - Golden
*Tigereye - Red
Topaz
Tourmaline
Triphylite
Turquoise
Unikite
*Variscite
*Whillolkite
*Wolfeite
*Yekem

*Photos in this section

Included in the listing is a man-made mineral that has been in use for 100 years, primarily for jewelry making. However, it does produce a striking marble. That mineral is goldstone. It comes in brown, blue, and more recently, purple. It is a beautiful material full of thousands of sparkles. See photo numbers I-170 through I-175.

Mineral and Stone Variations

Natural Agate

Size	Mint	Near Mint
1/2" - 3/4"	$8-12	$4-8
13/16" - 1-1/8"	$15-25	$8-15
Over 1-1/8"	$25-50	$15-30

Banded, Natural Agate

Size	Mint	Near Mint
1/2" - 3/4"	$15-30	$10-15
13/16" - 1-1/8"	$25-60	$15-25
Over 1-1/8"	$40-75	$25-40

Dyed Banded Agate

Size	Mint	Near Mint
1/2" - 3/4"	$75-150	$30-75
13/16" - 1-1/8"	$100-200	$40-100
Over 1-1/8"	$150-300	$80-150

Other Minerals and Stone

Size	Mint	Near Mint
1/2" - 3/4"	$15-30	$8-15
13/16" - 1-1/8"	$30-60	$15-30
Over 1-1/8"	$40-80	$30-50

All of the above are subjective to coloring and eye appeal.

Note: Semi precious minerals would have a multiple of 2x to 5x the above figures. Other rare minerals or combinations of minerals would have a multiple of 2x to 4x the above figures. Modern cut minerals and stone would have a reduction of 1/3 to 2/3 the above figures.

I-1. Natural and dyed agate. *Collection of Mark Block.*

I-2. Natural and dyed agate.

I-3. Carnelian agate, 3/4" d.

I-4. Carnelian agate, 3/4" d.

I-5. Carnelian agate, 11/16" d.

I-6. Carnelian agate, 11/16" d. Reverse of #5.

I-7. Carnelian agate, 11/16" d.

I-8. Banded agate, 11/16" d.

I-9. Banded agate, 11/16" d. Reverse of #8.

I-10. Banded aggregate, 3/4" d. Top view.

I-11. Banded aggregate, 3/4" d. Side view #10.

I-12. Banded aggregate, 3/4" d. Reverse of #10.

I-13. Banded aggregate, 13/16" d.

I-14. Banded agate, 1" d.

I-15. Banded agate, 1" d. Side view of #14.

I-16. Banded agate, 1" d. Reverse of #14.

I-17. Banded agate, 15/16" d.

I-18. Banded agate, 15/16" d. End view of #17.

I-19. Banded agate, 15/16" d. End view.

I-20. Banded agate, 15/16" d. Side view of #19.

I-21. Banded agate, 15/16" d.

I-22. Banded agate, 15/16" d. Reverse of #21.

I-23. Banded agate, 7/8" d.

I-24. Banded agate, 3/4" d.

I-25. Banded agate, 3/4" d. Reverse of #24.

I-26. Banded agate, 7/8" d.

I-27. Banded agate, 7/8" d. Side view of #26.

I-28. Banded agate, 3/4" d.

I-29. Banded agate, 3/4" d. Side view of #28.

I-30. Banded agate, 3/4" d.

I-31. Banded agate, 1" d.

I-32. Banded agate, 1" d. Reverse of #31.

I-33. Banded agate, 3/4" d.

I-34. Banded agate, 3/4" d.

I-35. Banded agate, 3/4" d. Side view of #34.

I-36. Banded agate, 3/4" d. End view of #34.

I-37. Banded agate, 15/16" d.

I-38. Banded agate, 15/16". Side view of #37.

I-39. Banded agate, 3/4" d.

I-40. Banded agate, 3/4" d. Side view of #39.

I-41. Banded agate, 11/16" d.

I-42. Banded agate, 1" d.

I-43. Banded agate, 1" d. Side view of #42.

I-44. Banded agate, 5/8" d. Side view.

I-45. Banded agate, 5/8" d. End view of #44.

I-46. Banded agate, 3/4" d. Side view.

I-47. Banded agate, 3/4" d. End view of #46.

I-48. Banded agate with Owl's Eyes, 3/4" d.

I-49. Banded agate with Owl's Eyes, 3/4" d. Side view.

I-50. Banded agate with Owl's Eyes, 3/4" d. Reverse of #48.

I-51. Banded agate with Owl's Eyes, 3/4" d. Opposite end of #48.

I-52. Banded agate, 3/4" d.

I-53. Banded agate, 11/16" d.

I-54. Banded agate, 11/16" d. End view of #53.

I-55. Banded agate, 5/8" d. Side view.

I-56. Banded agate, 5/8" d.

I-57. Banded agate, 5/8" d. End view.

I-58. Banded agate, 5/8" d. Side view of #57.

I-59. Banded agate, 11/16" d. End view.

I-60. Banded agate, 11/16" d. Side view of #59.

I-61. Banded agate, 9/16" d. Side view.

I-62. Banded agate, 9/16" d. End view of #61.

I-63. Banded agate, 9/16" d.

I-64. Banded agate, 9/16" d. Reverse of #63.

I-65. Banded agate, 9/16" d.

I-66. Banded agate, 9/16" d. Reverse of #65.

I-67. Banded agate, 9/16" d.

I-68. Banded agate, 9/16" d. Side view of #67.

I-69. Banded agate with Owl's Eyes, 13/16" d.

I-70. Banded agate with Owl's Eyes, 13/16" d. Side view of #69.

I-71. Banded agate, 11/16" d.

I-72. Banded agate, 11/16" d. Side view of #71.

I-73. Banded agate, 11/16" d. Side view.

I-74. Banded agate, 11/16" d. End view of #73.

I-75. Banded agate, 9/16" d.

I-76. Banded agate, 9/16" d. Side view of #75.

I-77. Banded agate, 9/16" d.

I-78. Banded agate, 9/16" d. Side view of #77.

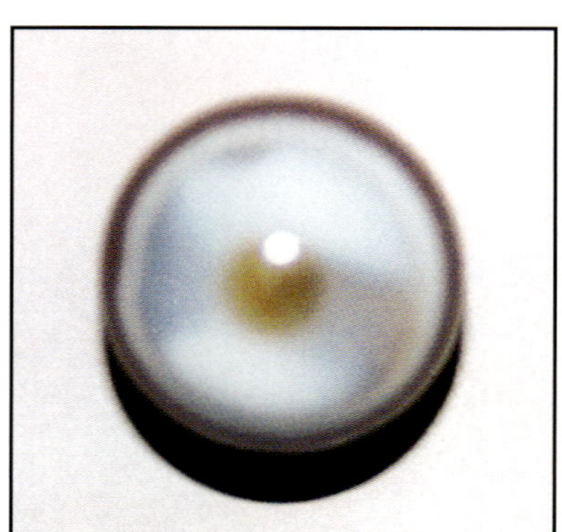

I-79. Banded agate, 9/16" d.

I-80. Banded agate, 9/16" d. Reverse of #79.

I-81. Banded agate, 9/16" d. Side view.

I-82. Banded agate, 9/16" d. End view of #81.

I-83. Banded agate, 1-1/4" d.

I-84. Banded agate with onyx, 1-5/8" d.

I-85. Banded agate, box top and bottom, with agate marble feet.

I-86. Natural and dyed banded agate necklace. *Collection of Jeff Yale.*

I-87. Dyed banded agate, 7/8" d.

I-88. Dyed banded agate, 15/16" d.

I-89. Dyed banded agate, 15/16" d. Top view of #88.

I-90. Dyed banded agate, 7/8" d. Side view.

I-91. Dyed banded agate, top and side of #90

I-92. Dyed banded agate, 15/16" d. Side view.

I-93. Dyed banded agate, 15/16" d. Reverse of #92.

I-94. Dyed banded agate, 13/16" d. End view.

I-95. Dyed banded agate, 13/16" d. Side view of #94.

I-96. Dyed banded agate, 15/16" d.

I-97. Dyed banded agate, 15/16" d. Side view of #96.

I-98. Dyed banded agate, 15/16" d. Side view.

I-99. Dyed banded agate, 15/16" d. Top view of #98.

I-100. Dyed banded agate, 7/8" d. Side view.

I-101. Dyed banded agate, 7/8" d. End view of #100.

I-102. Dyed banded agate, 13/16" d. Top view.

I-103. Dyed banded agate, 13/16" d. Side view of #102.

I-104. Dyed banded agate, 7/8" d.

I-105. Dyed banded agate, 7/8" d. Side view of #104.

I-106. Dyed banded agate, 7/8" d.

I-107. Dyed banded agate, 7/8" d. End view of #106.

I-108. Dyed banded agate, 5/8" d.

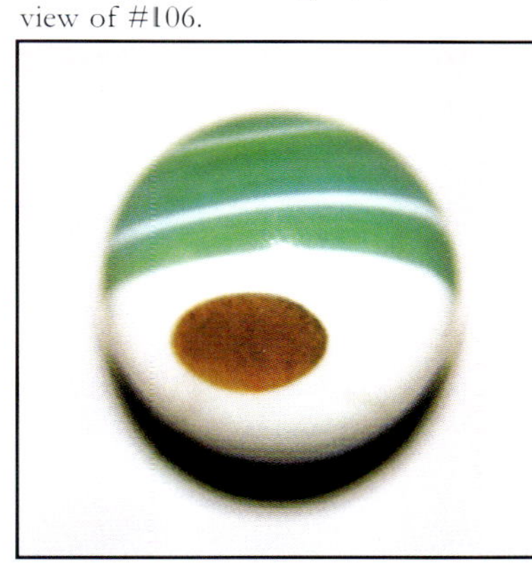

I-109. Dyed banded agate, 5/8" d. Side view of #108.

I-110. Dyed banded agate, 5/8" d.

I-111. Dyed banded agate, 1/2" d.

I-112. Dyed banded agate, 1/2" d. Side view of #111.

I-113. Dyed banded agate, 11/16" d.

I-114. Dyed banded agate, 11/16" d. Side view of #113.

I-115. Dyed banded agate, 5/8" d.

I-116. Dyed banded agate, 5/8" d. Side view of #115.

I-117. Dyed banded agate, 11/16" d.

I-118. Dyed banded agate, 11/16" d. Side view of #117.

I-119. Dyed banded agate, 9/16" d. Side view.

I-120. Dyed banded agate, 9/16" d. Reverse side of #119.

I-121. Dyed banded agate, 9/16" d. Top view of #119.

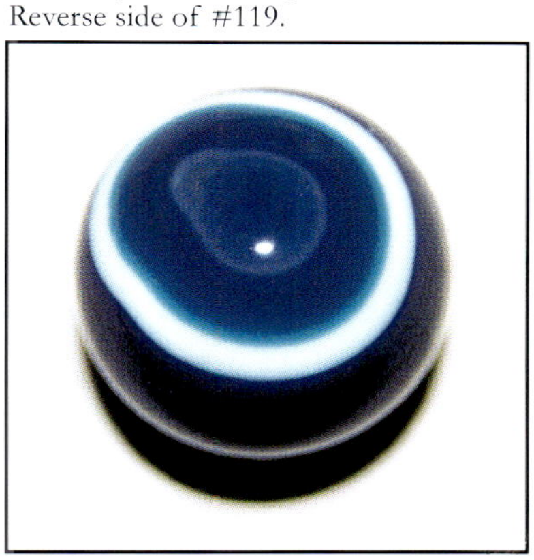

I-122. Dyed banded agate, 11/16" d. Top view.

I-123. Dyed banded agate, 11/16" d. Side view of #122.

I-124. Dyed banded agate, 1" d. Top view.

I-125. Dyed banded agate, 1" d. Side view of #124.

I-126. Dyed banded agate, 3/4" d. End view.

I-127. Dyed banded agate, 3/4" d. Side view of #126.

I-128. Dyed banded agate, 9/16" d.

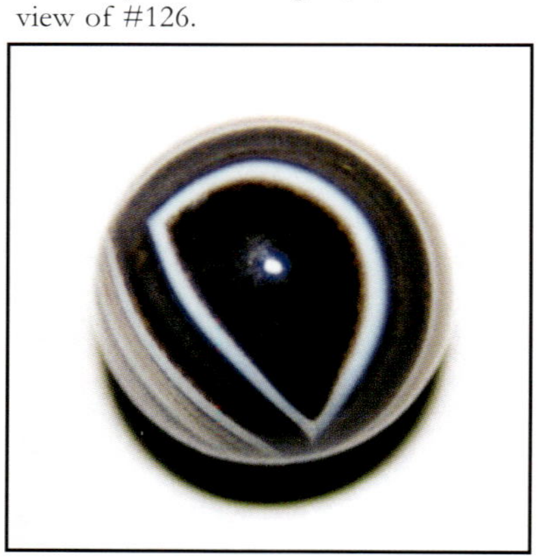

I-129. Dyed banded agate, 9/16" d. Top view of #128.

I-130. Dyed banded agate, 9/16" d. Side view of #128.

I-131. Dyed banded agate, 5/8" d. Top view.

I-132. Dyed banded agate, 5/8" d. Side view of #131.

I-133. Dyed banded agate, 11/16" d. Top view.

I-134. Dyed banded agate, 11/16" d. Side view of #133.

I-135. Dyed banded agate, 11/16" d.

I-136. Dyed banded agate, 11/16" d. Reverse of #135.

I-137. Dyed banded agate, 11/16" d.

I-138. Dyed banded agate, 9/16" d. Rare color.

I-139. Dyed banded agate, 9/16" d. Side view of #138.

I-140. Dyed banded agate, 9/16" d. Reverse of #139.

I-141. Dyed banded agate, 1-1/4" d. Side view.

I-142. Dyed banded agate, 1-1/4" d. Top view of #141.

I-143. Dyed banded agate, 1-1/4" d. Top view.

I-144. Dyed banded agate, 1-1/4" d. Side view of #143.

I-145. Lace agate, 15/16" d.

I-146. Lace agate, 15/16" d. Reverse of #145.

I-147. Lace agate, 13/16" d. End view.

I-148. Lace agate, 13/16" d. Reverse of #147.

I-149. Crazy lace agate, 1-1/2". *Collection of Mark Block.*

I-150. Crazy lace agate, 1".

I-151. Picture agate, 1".

I-152. Picture agate, 1".

I-153. Picture agate, 1". Reverse of #152.

I-154. Group of various minerals.

I-155. Amethyst, 15/16".

I-156. Amethyst, 15/16". Reverse of #155.

I-157. Angelite, 13/16".

I-158. Aragonite, 2". *Collection of John Medici.*

I-159. Aventurine, 11/16".

I-160. Aventurine, 3/4".

I-161. Aventurine, 11/16".

I-162. Bloodstone, 1-1/4".

I-163. Bloodstone, 1-1/4". Reverse of #162.

I-164. Bloodstone, 1-1/4".

I-165. Chert, 1-1/2". *Courtesy of John Medici.*

I-166. Chrysocola, 13/16".

I-167. Fluorite, 3/4".

I-168. Fluorite, 3/4".

I-169. Fluorite, 13/16".

I-170. Goldstone, 15/16".

I-171. Goldstone, 15/16".

I-172. Goldstone, 15/16".

I-173. Blue goldstone, 15/16".

I-174. Goldstone, 15/16".

I-175. Goldstone, 15/16". Reverse of #174.

I-176. Granite, 15/16".

I-177. Granite, 2".

I-178. Howlite, 11/16".

I-179. Jade, 9/16".

I-180. Jade, 1/2".

I-181. Jasper, 13/16".

I-182. Jasper, 13/16". Reverse of #181.

I-183. Jasper, 3/4".

I-184. Jasper, 1-1/8". *Collection of Mark Block.*

I-185. Jasper, 3/4".

I-186. Jasper, 3/4".

I-187. Jasper, 3/4". Reverse of #186.

I-188. Jasper, 3/4".

I-189. Jasper, 3/4". Reverse of #188.

I-190. Jasper, 3/4".

I-191. Jasper, 13/16".

I-192. Jasper, 13/16". Reverse of #191.

I-193. Jasper, 1".

I-194. Ocean jasper (a.k.a. Eye agate), 1-3/4". *Collection of John Medici.*

I-195. Poppy jasper, 1-1/16". *Collection of John Medici.*

I-196. Lapis Lazuli, 1-1/8".

I-197. Lapis Lazuli, 1-1/8". Reverse of #196.

I-198. Lapis Lazuli, 1-1/8". End view of #196.

I-199. Lapis Lazuli, 13/16".

I-200. Lapis Lazuli, 13/16". Reverse of #199.

I-201. Lapis Lazuli, 3/4".

I-202. Lapis Lazuli, 3/4". Reverse of #201.

I-203. Leopard skin, 7/8".

I-204. Leopard skin, 7/8". Side view of #203.

I-205. Leopard skin, 1-7/8".

I-206. Malachite, 7/8". Side view.

I-207. Malachite, 15/16".

I-208. Malachite, 1-5/8".

I-209. Malachite, 1-5/8". Reverse of #208.

I-210. Malachite, 9/16".

I-211. Malachite, 9/16". Side view of #210.

I-212. Obicular, 1-3/4".

I-213. Obicular, 1-3/4". Reverse of #212.

I-214. Obsidian, 2".

I-215. Mahogany obsidian, 2-1/8".
Collection of Mark Block.

I-216. Black onyx, 1-3/4".

I-217. Onyx, 3/4".

I-218. Onyx, 3/4". Reverse of #217.

I-219. Opal, 13/16".

I-220. Petrified palm, 7/8".

I-221. Petrified palm, 7/8".

I-222. Petrified palm, 7/8". Reverse of #221.

I-223. Porphyry, 1-1/2".

I-224. Optical quartz, 7/8".

I-225. Smoky quartz, 7/8".

I-226. Rose quartz, 1".

I-227. Rutilated quartz, 15/16".

I-228. Rutilated quartz, 15/16".

I-229. Rose quartz, 1".

I-230. Rhodochrosite, 13/16".

I-231. Rhodochrosite, 13/16". Reverse of #230.

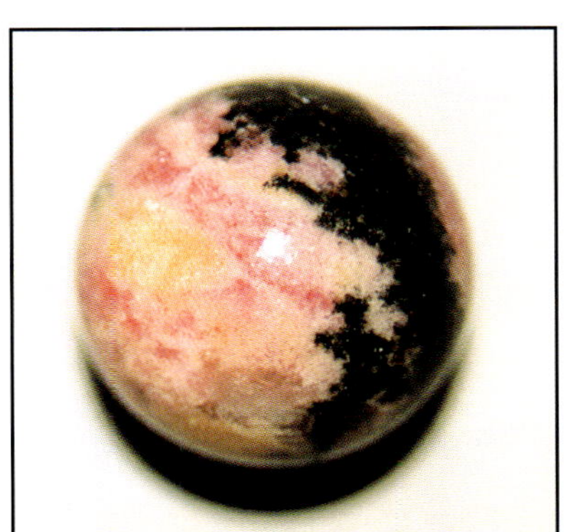

I-232. Rhodonite, 15/16".

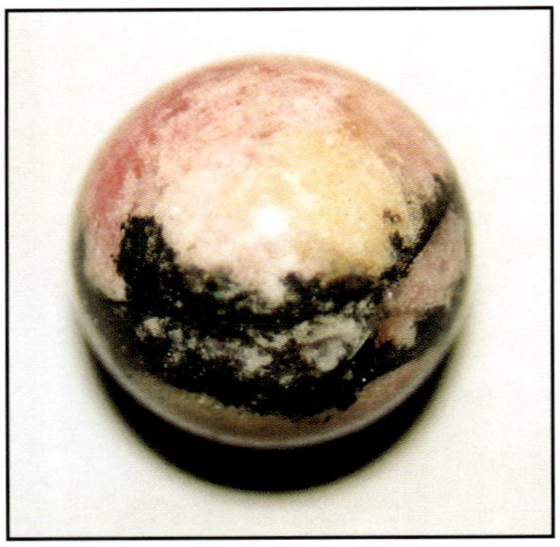

I-233. Rhodenite, 15/16". Reverse of #232.

I-234. Rhodenite, 7/8".

I-235. Rhodenite, 7/8". Reverse of #234.

I-236. Star ruby (man-made), 1/2".

I-237. Star sapphire (man-made), 1/2".

I-238. Serpentine, 1".

I-239. Sodalite, 13/16".

I-240. Sodalite, 13/16". Reverse of #239.

I-241. Stromatolite, 2". *Collection of John Medici.*

I-242. Golden tiger-eye, 1".

I-243. Golden tiger-eye, 2". Reverse of #242.

I-244. Golden tiger-eye, 1-1/4".

I-245. Golden tiger-eye, 1-1/4". Reverse of #244.

I-246. Golden tiger-eye, 1-1/2".

I-247. Red tiger-eye, 7/8".

I-248. Red tiger-eye, 7/8". Reverse of #247.

I-249. Red tiger-eye, 1".

I-250. Red tiger-eye, 1". Reverse of #249.

I-251. Red tiger-eye, 13/16".

I-252. Red tiger-eye, 13/16". Reverse of #251.

I-253. Tiger iron, 7/8".

I-254. Blue tiger-eye, 1".

I-255. Variscite, 13/16".

I-256. Yekem, 1".

I-257. Variscite, 1-9/16". *Collection of John Medici.*

I-258. Scorzalite, whillockite, and wolfite, 1-7/8". *Collection of John Medici.*

Section II: Clay, Crockery, and Pottery

Following the stream tumbled stone marbles, clays are the next oldest variety. Examples have been found in ancient Egyptian tombs and archaeological digs. Recently it was announced that more than ten clay marbles dating from the Ilkhanid Era (1251-1355) were discovered at a site in West Azerbaijan.

Clays are the easiest to produce and billions have been made and sold during the last 200 years in both the United States and Germany. One U.S. company packaged them to sell by the bag full, with 1,000 clay marbles to the bag. Clays come in a variety of colors depending on the type of clay used. Most common are shades of brown and gray. Large quantities were also dyed with shades of red, green, yellow, blue, purple or brown, as well as with mottled colors. Of all of the types of marbles, clays and crockeries were the least expensive.

Crockery was usually made of finer, whiter materials and was denser than clay. Some of the crockery marbles were decorated and some were also glazed. They can be found in any combination. In the same category are lined crockery, pottery, and earthenware.

The most plentiful of these latter varieties are "Bennington" Pottery Marbles. Although the U.S. company with that name cannot find any records of ever having sold "Bennington" marbles, the marbles have the same characteristics and look of Bennington Pottery items. It should also be noted that boxes of this type of pottery marble were imported from Germany and were listed in early toy sections of mail order catalogues.

The most common "Bennington" marbles are dyed blue or brown. Harder to find colors are green, black, or yellow. The base marble starts out white or in rare cases pink or red. To the base marble the color and final glaze are fired on. There are also "Fancy Bennington's," which are multicolored examples. "Bennington's" are easily recognized by the "eyes" that are found on the surface. The "eyes" are spots on the marble that are formed and fired in place when the marbles leaned against each other during the firing process.

See photo numbers II-24 through II-99 for various colors and combinations and for the "eyes." Photo number II-37 is an original box imported from Germany around the turn of the last century. It is stamped "Made in Germany" and has a paper label marked "Agates-Imitation."

Lined Crockery is a popular collectible. The more elaborate the lining or the rarer the colored lines, the higher the prices will be. See photo numbers II-104 through II-152.

Stoneware and Earthenware Pottery marbles can have applied dyes and designs fired on the surface and sometimes glazed over.

Spongeware is one of these, and is highly sought after by collectors. Sizes of marbles in this section can range from peewees (1/2" diameter) to well over 2" diameter. See photo numbers II-158 through II-199. At this point, we should mention Ballot Box marbles. These marbles have been made of china, clay, pottery, and glass. Close examination of these marbles with a bright light can usually show which material was used.

Contemporary artisans and craftsmen are making a variety of materials to produce modern versions of clay and pottery marbles. See photo numbers II-200 through II-230.

Children and their parents are also making clay marbles using products easily available such as Sculptey® Clay.

Section II:

Clays - Natural or Dyed

	Mint	Near Mint
1/2" to 3/4"	.02 - .20	.01 - .05
13/16" - 1-1/8"	.15-.30	.05-.10
Over 1-1/8"	$1-3	.50-1

Foil type - multiply 2x
Fancy dyes - multiply 3x

Crockery (Glazed)

1/2" - 3/4"	$2-10	.50-2
13/16" - 1-1/8"	$10-25	$5-10
Over 1-1/8"	$75-200	$20-50

Unglazed reduce by 1/4
Fancy types multiply 2x-3x

Pottery (Bennington Types)

1/2" - 3/4"	.25-.50	.10-.20
13/16" - 1-1/8"	.75-2	.50-1
Over 1-1/8" to 1-1/2"	$5-15	$2-5
Over 1-1/2"	$25-75	$10-20

Fancy types multiply 2x-3x
Red or pink based multiply 5x
Rarer colors multiply 3x
Modern types reduce by 1/2

Stoneware - Spongeware

1/2" - 3/4"	$10-25	$2-5
13/16" - 1-1/8"	$30-50	$10-20
Over 1-1/8" - 1-1/2"	$60-125	$30-50
Over 1-1/2"	$150-300	$30-80

Unusual designs multiply 3x

Mochaware

Spongeware multiply 2x-3x

II-1. Group of natural and dyed clay. *Collection of Robert Block.*

II-2. Natural clay, 3/4" d. *Collection of Robert Block.*

II-3. Natural clay, 3/4" d. *Collection of Robert Block.*

II-4. Dyed clay, 3/4" d. *Collection of Robert Block.*

II-5. Dyed clay, 7/8" d. *Collection of Robert Block.*

II-6. Dyed clay, 11/16" d. *Collection of Robert Block.*

II-7. Dyed clay, 11/16" d. *Collection of Robert Block.*

II-8. Dyed clay, 3/4" d. *Collection of Robert Block.*

II-9. Dyed clay, 5/8" d. *Collection of Robert Block.*

II-10. Dyed clay, 11/16" d. *Collection of Robert Block.*

II-11. Dyed clay, 5/8" d. *Collection of Robert Block.*

II-12. Dyed clay, 5/8" d. *Collection of Robert Block.*

II-13. Dyed clay, 11/16" d. *Collection of Robert Block.*

II-14. Dyed clay, 11/16" d. *Collection of Robert Block.*

II-15. Dyed clay, 11/16" d. *Collection of Robert Block.*

II-16. Dyed clay, 5/8" d. *Collection of Robert Block.*

II-17. Dyed clay, 11/16" d. *Collection of Robert Block.*

II-18. Box of German clays. *Collection of Robert Block.*

II-19. Box of German clays. Reverse side. *Collection of Robert Block.*

II-20. Mosaic game with foil clays. *Collection of Robert Block.*

II-21. Inside of mosaic game. *Collection of Robert Block.*

II-22. Tray of mosaic foil covered clays.
Collection of Robert Block.

II-23. Group of pottery and crockery.

II-24. Brown "Bennington" pottery, 1-1/2" d.

II-25. Brown "Bennington" pottery, 1-1/2" d. Reverse side of #24.

II-26. Brown "Bennington" pottery, 1" d.

II-27. Brown "Bennington" pottery, 1" d. Reverse of #26.

II-28. Brown "Bennington" pottery, 15/16" d.

II-29. Brown "Bennington" pottery, 15/16" d. Reverse of #28.

II-30. Brown "Bennington" pottery, 7/8" d.

II-31. Brown "Bennington" pottery, 7/8" d. Reverse of #30.

II-32. Brown "Bennington" pottery, 5/8" d.

II-33. Brown "Bennington" pottery, 7/8" d.

II-34. Brown "Bennington" pottery, 7/8" d. Reverse of #33.

II-35. Brown "Bennington" pottery, 13/16" d.

II-36. Brown "Bennington" pottery, 13/16" d. Reverse of #35.

II-37. Box of German "Bennington" pottery marbles.

II-38. Blue "Bennington" pottery, 1" d.

II-39. Blue "Bennington" pottery, 1" d. Reverse of #38.

II-40. Blue "Bennington" pottery, 7/8" d.

II-41. Blue "Bennington" pottery, 7/8" d. Reverse of #40.

II-42. Blue "Bennington" pottery, 1-1/8" d.

II-43. Blue "Bennington" pottery, 1-1/8" d. Reverse of #42.

II-44. Blue "Bennington" pottery, 5/8" d.

II-45. Blue "Bennington" pottery, 5/8" d. Reverse of #44.

II-46. Blue "Bennington" pottery, 5/8" d.

II-47. Blue "Bennington" pottery, 5/8" d. Reverse of #45.

II-48. Blue "Bennington" pottery, 5/8" d.

II-49. Blue "Bennington" pottery, 9/16" d.

II-50. Blue "Bennington" pottery, 9/16" d.

II-51. Blue "Bennington" pottery, 5/8" d.

II-52. Blue "Bennington" pottery, 5/8" d.

II-53. Blue "Bennington" pottery, 3/4" d.

II-54. Blue "Bennington" pottery, 11/16" d.

II-55. Blue "Bennington" pottery, 11/16" d. Reverse of #54.

II-56. Blue "Bennington" pottery, 9/16" d.

II-57. Blue "Bennington" pottery, 13/16" d.

II-58. Fancy "Bennington" pottery, 7/8" d.

II-59. Fancy "Bennington" pottery, 7/8" d. Reverse of #58.

II-60. Fancy "Bennington" pottery, 9/16" d.

II-61. Fancy "Bennington" pottery, 9/16" d. Reverse of #60.

II-62. Fancy "Bennington" pottery, 1-1/8" d.

II-63. Fancy "Bennington" pottery, 1-1/8" d. Reverse of #62.

II-64. Fancy "Bennington" pottery, 3/4" d.

II-65. Fancy "Bennington" pottery, 3/4" d. Reverse of #64.

II-66. Fancy "Bennington" pottery, 3/4" d.

II-67. Fancy "Bennington" pottery, 3/4" d. Reverse of #66.

II-68. Fancy "Bennington" pottery, 3/4" d. Side view of #66.

II-69. Fancy "Bennington" pottery, 3/4" d.

II-70. Fancy "Bennington" pottery, 3/4" d. Reverse of #69.

II-71. Fancy "Bennington" pottery, 3/4" d.

II-72. Fancy "Bennington" pottery, 3/4" d.

II-73. Fancy "Bennington" pottery, 7/8" d.

II-74. Fancy "Bennington" pottery, 5/8" d.

II-75. Fancy "Bennington" pottery, 11/16" d.

II-76. Fancy 'Bennington" pottery, 11/16" d. Reverse of #75.

II-77. Fancy "Bennington" pottery, 3/4" d.

II-78. Fancy 'Bennington" pottery, 5/8" d.

II-79. Fancy "Bennington" pottery, 9/16" d.

II-80. Fancy "Bennington" pottery, 9/16" d.

II-81. Fancy "Bennington" pottery, 5/8" d.

II-82. Fancy "Bennington" pottery, 13/16" d.

II-83. Fancy "Bennington" pottery, 13/16" d. Reverse of #82.

II-84. Fancy "Bennington" pottery, 13/16" d. Top view of #82.

II-85. Fancy "Bennington" pottery, 11/16" d.

II-86. Fancy "Bennington" pottery, 11/16" d. Reverse of #85

II-87. Fancy "Bennington" pottery, 5/8" d.

II-88. Fancy "Bennington" pottery, 5/8" d. Reverse of #87.

II-89. Fancy "Bennington" pottery, 13/16" d.

II-90. Fancy "Bennington" pottery, 1-1/8" d.

II-91. Fancy "Bennington" pottery, 1-1/8" d. Reverse of #90.

II-92. Fancy "Bennington" pottery, 1-1/8" d. Side view of #90.

II-93. Fancy "Bennington" pottery, 5/8" d.

II-94. Fancy "Bennington" pottery, 5/8" d. Reverse of #93.

II-95. Fancy "Bennington" pottery, 3/4" d.

II-96. Fancy "Bennington" pottery, 3/4" d. Reverse of #95.

II-97. Fancy "Bennington" pottery, 11/16" d.

II-98. Fancy paneled "Bennington" pottery, 5/8" d. *Collection of Jerry Biern.*

II-99. Fancy paneled "Bennington" pottery, 5/8" d. Reverse of #98. *Collection of Jerry Biern.*

II-100. Ballot box pottery marble, 9/16" d.

II-101. Ballot box pottery marble, 9/16" d. Reverse of #100.

II-102. Ballot box pottery marble, 9/16" d.

II-103. Ballot box pottery marble, 9/16" d. Reverse of #102.

II-104. Lined crockery, 21/32" d. *Collection of Jerry Biern.*

II-105. Lined crockery, 21/32" d. Reverse of #104. *Collection of Jerry Biern.*

II-106. Lined crockery, 21/32" d. *Collection of Jerry Biern.*

II-107. Lined crockery, 24/32" d. *Collection of Jerry Biern.*

II-108. Lined crockery, 23/32" d. *Collection of Jerry Biern.*

II-109. Lined crockery, 23/32" d. Reverse of #108. *Collection of Jerry Biern.*

II-110. Lined crockery, 5/8" d.

II-111. Lined crockery, 13/16" d.

II-112. Lined crockery, 13/16" d. Reverse of #111.

II-113. Glazed lined crockery, 13/16" d.

II-114. Glazed lined crockery, 13/16" d. Reverse of #113.

II-115. Glazed lined pottery, 23/32" d. *Collection of Jerry Biern.*

II-116. Glazed lined pottery, 23/32" d. *Collection of Jerry Biern.*

II-117. Glazed lined pottery, 7/8" d.

II-118. Glazed lined pottery, 7/8" d.
Reverse of #117.

II-119. Glazed lined pottery, 11/16" d.

II-120. Glazed lined pottery, 11/16" d.
Reverse of #119.

II-121. Glazed lined pottery, 1" d.

II-122. Glazed lined pottery, 11/16" d.

II-123. Glazed lined pottery, 5/8" d.

II-124. Glazed lined pottery, 11/16" d.

II-125. Glazed lined pottery, 15/32" d.
Collection of Jerry Biern.

II-126. Glazed lined pottery, 15/32" d.
Collection of Jerry Biern.

II-127. Glazed lined pottery, 15/32" d.
Reverse of #126. *Collection of Jerry Biern.*

II-128. Glazed lined pottery, 9/16" d.

II-129. Glazed lined pottery, 9/16" d.
Reverse of #128.

II-130. Glazed lined pottery, 1" d.

II-131. Glazed lined pottery, 1" d. Reverse of #130.

II-132. Glazed lined pottery, 1" d. Side view of #130.

II-133. Glazed lined pottery, 13/16" d.

II-134. Glazed lined pottery, 3/4" d.

II-135. Glazed lined pottery, 3/4" d.

II-136. Glazed lined pottery, 3/4" d. Reverse of #135.

II-137. Glazed lined pottery, 1-1/8" d.

II-138. Glazed lined pottery, 1-1/8" d. Reverse of #137.

II-139. Glazed lined pottery, 3/4" d.

II-140. Glazed lined pottery, 3/4" d. Reverse of #139.

II-141. Glazed lined pottery, 13/16" d.

II-142. Glazed lined pottery, 13/16" d. Reverse of #141.

II-143. Glazed lined pottery, 11/16" d.

II-144. Glazed lined pottery, 5/8" d.

II-145. Glazed lined pottery, 5/8" d.
Reverse of #144.

II-146. Glazed lined pottery, 5/8" d.

II-147. Glazed lined pottery, 5/8" d.
Reverse of #146

II-148. Glazed lined pottery, 7/8" d.
Collection of Robert Block.

II-149. Glazed lined pottery, 7/8" d.
Reverse of #148. *Collection of Robert Block.*

II-150. Glazed lined pottery, 3/4" d.
Collection of Jerry Biern.

II-151. Glazed lined pottery, 3/4" d.
Reverse of #150. *Collection of Jerry Biern.*

II-152. Glazed lined pottery, 3/4" d. *Collection of Jerry Biern.*

II-154. Mocha ware. 2-1/4" d. *Collection of Jeff Yale.*

II-153. Glazed pottery group from Akron, Ohio. *Collection of Robert Block.*

II-155. Mocha ware. 2-1/8" d. *Collection of Jeff Yale.*

II-156. Mocha ware. 2-3/8" d. *Collection of Jeff Yale.*

II-157. Mocha ware. 2-3/8" d. Reverse of #156. *Collection of Jeff Yale.*

II-158. Spongeware, 1-5/8" d.

II-159. Spongeware, 1-5/8" d. Side view of #158.

II-160. Spongeware, 1-3/4" d.

II-161. Spongeware, 1-7/8" d.

II-162. Spongeware, 1-7/8" d. Reverse of #161.

II-163. Spongeware, 1-7/8" d. Side view of #161.

II-164. Spongeware, 11/16" d.

II-165. Spongeware, 11/16" d. Reverse of #164.

II-166. Spongeware, 1-3/8" d.

II-167. Spongeware, 15/16" d.

II-168. Spongeware, 15/16" d. Reverse of #167.

II-169. Spongeware, 3/4" d.

II-170. Spongeware, 15/16" d.

II-171. Spongeware, 15/16" d.

II-172. Spongeware, 15/16" d. Reverse of #171.

II-173. Spongeware, 15/16" d.

II-174. Spongeware, 15/16" d. Reverse of #173.

II-175. Spongeware, 1" d.

II-176. Spongeware, 1" d. Reverse of #175.

II-177. Spongeware, 1-1/4" d.

II-178. Spongeware, 1-1/4" d. Reverse of #177.

II-179. Spongeware, 11/16" d. Side view.

II-180. Spongeware, 11/16" d. End view of #179.

II-181. Spongeware, 11/16" d.

II-182. Spongeware, 11/16" d. Reverse of #181.

II-183. Spongeware, 7/8" d.

II-184. Spongeware, 7/8" d.

II-185. Spongeware, 7/8" d. Reverse of #184.

II-186. Spongeware, 15/16" d.

II-187. Spongeware, 1-1/8" d.

II-188. Spongeware, 15/16" d.

II-189. Spongeware, 15/16" d. Reverse of #188.

II-190. Spongeware, 1-1/8" d.

II-191. Spongeware, 1-1/8" d. Reverse of #190.

II-192. Spongeware, 15/16" d.

II-193. Spongeware, 9/16" d.

II-194. Spongeware, 9/16" d. Reverse of #193.

II-195. Spongeware, 9/16" d.

II-196. Spongeware, 9/16" d. Reverse of #195.

II-197. Spongeware, 7/8" d. *Collection of Robert Block.*

II-198. Spongeware, 7/8" d. *Collection of Robert Block.*

II-199. Spongeware, 7/8" d. End view of #198. *Collection of Robert Block.*

II-201. Modern clay. Side view. *Collection of Claire Block.*

II-200. Group of modern clays. *Collection of Claire Block.*

II-202. Modern clay. Top view of #201. *Collection of Claire Block.*

II-203. Modern clay. *Collection of Claire Block.*

II-204. Modern clay. *Collection of Claire Block.*

II-205. Modern Clay. *Collection of Claire Block.*

II-206. Modern Clay. *Collection of Claire Block.*

II-207. Modern Clay. *Collection of Claire Block.*

II-208. Modern Clay. *Collection of Claire Block.*

II-209. Modern Clay. *Collection of Claire Block.*

II-210. Modern Clay. *Collection of Claire Block.*

II-211. Modern pottery, 1-1/8" d.

II-212. Modern pottery, 1-5/8" d.

II-213. Modern pottery, 1-1/8" d.

II-214. Modern pottery, 1" d. *Collection of Nadine MacDonald.*

II-215. Modern pottery, 1" d. Reverse of #214. *Collection of Nadine MacDonald.*

II-216. Modern pottery, 2" d. *Collection of Nadine MacDonald.*

II-217. Modern pottery, 1-5/8" d.

II-218. Modern pottery, 1-1/2" d.

II-219. Modern pottery, 1-3/8" d.

II-220. Modern pottery, 1-3/8" d.

II-221. Modern pottery, 1-5/8" d.

II-222. Modern pottery, 7/8" d.

II-223. Modern pottery, 7/8" d.

II-224. Modern pottery, 15/16" d.

II-225. Modern pottery, 1" d.

II-226. Modern pottery, 1" d. Reverse of #225.

II-227. Modern pottery, 1-1/2" d.

II-228. Modern pottery, 1-1/2" d.

II-229. Modern pottery, 1-5/8" d.

II-230. Modern pottery, 1-1/2" d.

Section III: China and Porcelain

China and porcelain marbles terminology has been co-mingled since the nineteenth century. Now we have ceramics to add to this general area of co-mingling terminology. The materials used are fine white clays that are fired at very high temperatures to produce a dense white marble. Most of the types in this section are referred to as chinas, except for carpet balls (bowls), which are referred to as handpainted porcelain. According to the research by Carskadden and Gartley, "chinas" were first noted in a journal by an Indiana potter in December 1844 concerning a shipment made by the potter, which included nine (9) dozen carpet balls, 1500 pottery marbles, and 800 china marbles. A later entry in 1846 indicates a shipment of 800 painted chinas. Although it is possible these were the cheaper pipe clay marble types, the price seems to indicate they were the denser china type marbles. The earliest decorated china marbles found in Midwest archaeological excavations indicate their use came into being during the 1830s to 1860 period and continues thereafter.

Carpet Balls (Bowls) are generally believed to have originated during the early part of the twelfth century. Its major growth occurred during the eighteenth century in Scotland and Northern England. They were used in popular lawn and parlor games. Bocce is the Italian variation of carpet bowls.

Carpet balls came in sets of eight to twelve balls plus a jack ball. The sets usually had matched pairs of designs on the carpet balls while the jack ball was usually white. The sets also came in different sizes with the largest sets having 4" diameter balls. During the last twenty years, modern versions of carpet balls have been produced. Some of the new carpet balls are being decorated with the same patterns as the originals. Others are decorated hollow ceramic balls. There are also a large number of mineral spheres currently being processed in the same sizes as carpet balls.

China marbles may come in a variety of types and designs. Each may be glazed or unglazed. The types shown in this section include examples with:

Bird's feet
Bull's-eyes
Checker Board
Donut Eye
Flowered
Grapes and Vines
Helix
Leaves
Lined
Mottled
Pennsylvania Dutch
Pinwheels
Quadrants
Scenic
Spiraled

Bull's-eye chinas are usually one of two varieties, donut hole or solid holes. There may be three to eight bull's-eyes on a single marble. Bull's-eyes are also used individually as part of the design of other handpainted chinas. For example, scenic chinas have a bull's-eye at each pole of the marble.

Flowered chinas come in a variety of flower types and designs. Usually there is a matching flower on each side of the marble. When there is only one flower on one side, the opposite side will usually have a set of Bird's feet or a helix pattern.

Scenic chinas are basically of two types. Both have been handpainted over a glazed china marble, usually 1-1/4" to 1-1/2" in diameter. The first variety has a scene painted around the center of the marble with pinwheel designs at each pole (photo numbers III-256 through III-271). The second type has about two thirds of the marbles painted in a solid color (usually dark blue) with the balance of the surface painted with a scene, usually of humans, cherubs, flowers, etc. in the style of French paintings. Sometimes decorated with gilt leaves or vines, most of this type was used as cane or parasol handles. Later examples of this type were decorated by using decals for the scenes instead of handpainting them.

The Pennsylvania Dutch style handpainted chinas appear to be on a less dense china marble as they seem to be lighter and more porous. Also if a glaze was applied to the finished marble it has a very light glaze. Decorations range from stylized flowers to fleur de lis to patterns of designs rather than scenes or geometric patterns (see photo numbers III-240 through III-255). The best way to learn the distinct varieties of chinas is to review and study the photos in this section.

Photo numbers III-343 through III-361 will give the reader a general idea of the modern versions of chinas, porcelains, and ceramic marbles available. There are a great many modern craftsmen working on marbles of all types. A visit to any of the marble shows held around the country would be very educational and enlightening. For readers on computers, many marble sites are available for viewing.

While we are on the subject of chinas and porcelain marbles, we should cover the "Atlanta Porcelains." As the story goes, while preparing a site for the 1996 Olympics, a worker dug up a wheelbarrow full of porcelain type marbles. They were a plain off-white color with surface crazing, but were very dense marbles, making them much heavier than old porcelain and china marbles of the same size. Over the years that wheelbarrow full has grown to carloads. First, dyed examples have appeared. More recently, painted and stenciled varieties have also been made available in growing numbers. It is this author's opinion that the first group had little collector value. The more recent appearing marbles have little or no collector value, and are probably being produced as this book is being written.

Chinas and Porcelain
Chinas Lined and Glazed

	Mint	Near Mint
1/2" - 3/4"	$10-20	$2-10
13/16" - 1-1/8"	$25-75	$15-30
Over 1-1/8" - 1-1/2"	$80-200	$25-50
Over 1-1/2"	$200-400	$50-100

Unglazed reduce by 1/4
Fancy lines or Helix 2x
Bull's-eyes 2x
Flowers on one side 5x
Flowers on both sides 10x
Intricate or Rarer Designs 15x
Scenic with Pinwheels 50x
PA Dutch style 25x
Handle type 15x

Carpet Bowls

1-1/2" - 2-1/4"	$100-200	$40-80
over 2-1/4"	$150-300	$75-100

Mocha Ware design types 5x
Jack Balls reduce by 1/2
Advertising types add 1/2
Rarer Designs and Coloring 2x-5x
Modern reduce by 3/4

III-1 Group photo - group of various Chinas.

III-2. Group photo - group of Bull's-eye Chinas.

III-3. Bull's-eye china, 3/4" d.

III-4. Bull's-eye china, 3/4" d. Reverse of #3.

III-5. Bull's-eye china, 11/16" d.

III-6. Bull's-eye china, 11/16" d. Reverse of #5.

III-7. Bull's-eye china, 3/4" d.

III-8. Bull's-eye china, 3/4" d. Reverse of #7.

III-9. Bull's-eye china, 3/4" d.

III-10. Bull's-eye china, 3/4" d. Reverse of #9.

III-11. Bull's-eye china, 3/4" d.

III-12. Bull's-eye china, 3/4" d. Reverse of #11.

III-13. Bull's-eye china, 11/16" d.

III-14. Bull's-eye china, 11/16" d.

III-15. Bull's-eye china, 1" d.

III-16. Bull's-eye china, 1" d. Reverse of #15.

III-17. Bull's-eye china in quadrants, 3/4" c. Side view. *Collection of Wayne Sanders.*

III-18. Bull's-eye china in quadrants, 3/4" d. End view of #17. *Collection of Wayne Sanders.*

III-19. Bull's-eye china, 3/4" d. *Collection of Hansel DeSousa.*

III-20. Bull's-eye china, 11/16" d. *Collection of Hansel DeSousa.*

III-21. Bull's-eye china, 7/8" d.

III-22. Bull's-eye china, 5/8" d.

III-23. Bull's-eye china, 3/4" d

III-24. Bull's-eye china, 7/8" d.

III-25. Bull's-eye china, 9/16" d.

III-26. Bull's-eye china, 9/16" d. Reverse of #25.

III-27. Bull's-eye china, 3/4" d.

III-28. Bull's-eye china, 3/4" d. Reverse of #27.

III-29. Bull's-eye china, 3/4" d.

III-30. Bull's-eye china, 3/4" d. Reverse of #29.

III-31. Bull's-eye china, 11/16" d.

III-32. Bull's-eye china, 3/4" d.

III-33. Bull's-eye china, 3/4" d. Reverse of #32.

III-34. Bull's-eye china, 11/16" d.

III-35. Bull's-eye china, 11/16" d.

III-36. Bull's-eye china, 3/4" d.

III-37. Bull's-eye china, 11/16" d.

III-38. Bull's-eye china, 5/8" d. *Collection of Jerry Biern.*

III-39. Bull's-eye china, 5/8" d. Reverse of #38. *Collection of Jerry Biern.*

III-40. Bull's-eye china with leaves, 3/4" d.

III-41. Bull's-eye china with leaves, 3/4" d. End view of #40.

III-42. Bull's-eye china with leaves, 3/4" d. Side view of #40.

III-43. Bull's-eye china with leaves, 3/4" d.

III-44. Bull's-eye china with leaves, 3/4" d. Side view of #43.

III-45. Bull's-eye china with leaves, 3/4" d.

III-46. Bull's-eye china with leaves, 13/16" d.

III-47. Bull's-eye china with leaves, 13/16" d. Side view of #46.

III-48. Bull's-eye china with leaves, 3/4" d.

III-49. Bull's-eye china with leaves, 3/4" d. End view of #48.

III-50. Bull's-eye china with blue berries, 5/8" d. End view. *Collection of Jerry Biern.*

III-51. Bull's-eye china with blue berries, 5/8" d. Side view. *Collection of Jerry Biern.*

III-52. Unglazed lined china, 11/16" d. *Collection of Jerry Biern.*

III-53. Unglazed lined china, 11/16" d. Reverse of #52. *Collection of Jerry Biern.*

III-54. Unglazed lined china, 11/16" d.

III-55. Glazed lined china, 1-1/4" d.

III-56. Glazed lined china, 1-1/4" d. Reverse of #55.

III-57. Unglazed lined china, 1-3/8" d.

III-58. Unglazed lined china, 1-3/8" d. Reverse of #57.

III-59. Glazed lined china, 3/4" d.

III-60. Glazed lined china, 11/16" d.

III-61. Glazed lined china, 11/16" d. Reverse of #60.

III-62. Glazed lined china, 3/4" d.

III-63. Glazed lined china, 3/4" d. Side view of #62.

III-64. Unglazed lined china, 11/16" d.

III-65. Unglazed lined china, 11/16" d. Side view of #64.

III-66. Unglazed lined china, 13/16" d.

III-67. Unglazed lined china, 13/16" d. Side view of #66.

III-68. Unglazed lined china, 13/16" d.

III-69. Unglazed lined china, 13/16" d.

III-70. Unglazed lined china, 13/16" d. Side view of #69.

III-71. Glazed lined china, 11/16" d.

III-72. Glazed lined china, 11/16" d. Side view of #71.

III-73. Glazed lined china, 9/16" d.

III-74. Glazed lined china, 9/16" d.
Side view of #73.

III-75. Glazed lined china, 13/16" d.

III-76. Glazed lined china, 7/8" d.

III-77. Glazed lined china, 11/16" d.

III-78. Glazed lined china, 11/16" d.
Reverse of #77.

III-79. Glazed lined china, 9/16" d.

III-80. Unglazed lined china, 3/4" d.

III-81. Unglazed lined china, 3/4" d.
Reverse of #80.

III-82. Glazed lined china, 11/16" d.

III-83. Glazed lined china, 11/16" d.
Reverse of #82.

III-84. Glazed lined china, 9/16" d.

III-85. Unglazed lined china, 5/8" d.

III-86. Unglazed lined china, 5/8" d.
Reverse of #85.

III-87. Glazed lined china, 9/16" d.

III-88. Glazed lined china, 9/16" d. Reverse of #87.

III-89. Glazed lined china, 9/16" d.

III-90. Glazed lined china, 9/16" d. Reverse of #89.

III-91. Glazed lined china, 9/16" d.

III-92. Glazed lined china, 11/16" d.

III-93. Glazed lined china, 11/16" d. Reverse of #92.

III-94. Glazed lined china, 11/16" d.

III-95. Glazed lined china, 11/16" d. Reverse of #94.

III-96. Glazed lined china, 9/16" d.

III-97. Glazed lined china, 5/8" d.

III-98. Unglazed lined china, 3/4" d.

III-99. Unglazed lined china, 11/16" d.

III-100. Unglazed lined china, 11/16" d.

III-101. Unglazed lined china, 11/16" d.
Reverse of #100.

III-102. Unglazed lined china, 3/4" d.

III-103. Unglazed lined china, 3/4" d.

III-104. Unglazed lined china, 3/4" d.
Reverse of #103.

III-105. Unglazed lined china, 7/8" d.

III-106. Unglazed lined china, 7/8" d.

III-107. Unglazed lined china, 7/8" d.
Reverse of #106.

III-108. Unglazed lined china, 1" d. with leaves at quadrants.

III-109. Unglazed lined china, 1" d. Reverse of #108.

III-110. Glazed lined china, 23/32" d. with leaves. *Collection of Jerry Biern.*

III-111. Glazed lined china, 23/32" d. Reverse of #110. *Collection of Jerry Biern.*

III-112. Glazed lined china, 3/4" d. *Collection of Jerry Biern.*

III-113. Glazed lined china, 3/4" d. with leaves. *Collection of Jeff Yale.*

III-114. Glazed lined china, 3/4" d. Reverse of #113. *Collection of Jeff Yale.*

III-115. Glazed lined china, 7/8" d. with leaves. *Collection of Jeff Yale.*

III-116. Glazed lined china, 1-1/2" d., four quadrants with leaves. *Collection of Jerry Biern.*

III-117. Glazed lined china with circular rings. 1-5/8" d.

III-118. Glazed lined china with circular rings. 1-5/8" d. Side view of #117.

III-119. Glazed lined china with circular rings. 1-5/8" d. End view of #117.

III-120. Glazed lined china with Bull's-eyes, rings, and leaves. 23/32" d. *Collection of Jerry Biern.*

III-121. Glazed lined china with Bull's-eyes, rings, and leaves. 21/32" d. Side view of #120. *Collection of Jerry Biern.*

III-122. Glazed china with helix and leaves, 1-1/8" d.

III-123. Glazed china with helix and leaves, 1-1/4" d.

III-124. Glazed china with helix and leaves, 1-1/4" d. Side view of #123.

III-125. Glazed china with helix and leaves, 1-3/8" d.

III-126. Glazed china with helix and leaves, 1-3/8" d. Side view of #125.

III-127. Glazed china with helix and leaves, 1-3/8" d. End view of #125.

III-128. Glazed china with helix and leaves, 3/4" d.

III-129. Glazed china with helix and leaves, 3/4" d.

III-130. Glazed china with helix, 9/16" d.

III-131. Glazed china with helix, 1-3/8" d. *Collection of Jeff Yale.*

III-132. Glazed china with helix and leaves, 11/15" d.

III-133. Glazed china with helix and leaves, 5/8" d.

III-134. Glazed china with helix and leaves, 5/8" d. Reverse of #133.

III-135. Glazed china with helix and leaves, 9/16" d.

III-136. Glazed china with helix and leaves, 9/16" d. Reverse of #135.

III-137. Glazed china with helix and leaves, 9/16" d.

III-138. Glazed china with helix and leaves, 9/16" d. Reverse of #137.

III-139. Glazed china with helix and leaves, 9/16" d.

III-140. Glazed china with helix and leaves, 9/16" d. Reverse of #139.

III-141. Glazed china with helix and leaves, 9/16" d.

III-142. Glazed china with helix and leaves, 9/16" d. Reverse of #141.

III-143. Glazed china with helix and leaves, 5/8" d.

III-144. Glazed china with helix and leaves, 11/15" d.

III-146. Group of glazed flower Chinas. *Collection of Peter Sharrer.*

III-145. Glazed china with helix and leaves, 1-1/4" d.

III-147. Glazed stylized flower china, 3/4" d.

III-148. Glazed stylized flower china, 3/4" d. Reverse of #147.

III-149. Glazed stylized flower china, 3/4" d. Side view of #147.

III-150. Glazed flower china, 11/16" d.

III-151. Glazed flower china, 11/16" d. Side view of #150.

III-152. Glazed donut or Bull's-eye stylized flower china, 11/16" d.

III-153. Glazed donut or Bull's-eye style flower china, 11/16" d. Side view of #152.

III-154. Unglazed four quadrant flowers, 3/4" d. Side view.

III-155. Unglazed four quadrant flowers, 3/4" d. Top view of #154.

III-156. Glazed Bull's-eye or donut style flower, 7/8" d.

III-157. Glazed rose style flower china, 1-1/8" d.

III-158. Glazed rose style flower china, 1-1/8" d. Side view of #157.

III-159. Glazed tulip style flower china, 3/4" d.

III-160. Glazed tulip style flower china, 3/4" d. Reverse of #159.

III-161. Unglazed dot petaled flower, 5/8" d. *Collection of Jerry Biern.*

III-162. Unglazed dot petaled flower, 5/8" d. Reverse of #161. *Collection of Jerry Biern.*

III-163. Unglazed donut flower, 15/16" d.

III-164. Glazed five petal flower, 1-1/8" d.

III-165. Unglazed shamrock, 5/8" d. *Collection of Jerry Biern.*

III-166. Unglazed shamrock, 5/8" d. Reverse of #165. *Collection of Jerry Biern.*

III-167. Rose china with pinwheel poles, 1-1/4" d. *Collection of Jerry Biern.*

III-168. Rose china with pinwheel poles, 1-1/4" d. Top and sides. *Collection of Jerry Biern.*

III-169. Rose china with pinwheel poles, 1-1/4" d. Side view of #167. *Courtesy of Jerry Biern.*

III-170. Unglazed flower china, 13/16" d. *Collection of Peter Sharrer.*

III-171. Unglazed flower china, 13/16" d. Reverse of #170. *Collection of Peter Sharrer.*

III-172. Unglazed five petal blue flower china, 13/16" d. *Collection of Peter Sharrer.*

III-173. Unglazed five petal blue flower china, 13/16" d. Reverse of #172. *Collection of Peter Sharrer.*

III-174. Unglazed five dot petaled flower china, 3/4" d. *Collection of Peter Sharrer.*

III-175. Unglazed five dot petaled flower china, 3/4" d. Reverse of #174. *Collection of Peter Sharrer.*

III-176. Unglazed rose china, 9/16" d. *Collection of Peter Sharrer.*

III-177. Glazed double pinwheel poles with central panel of grapes on vines, 1-3/8" d. *Collection of Auction Block.*

III-178. Glazed double pinwheel poles with central panel of grapes on vines, 1-3/8" d. Side view of #177. *Collection of Auction Block.*

III-179. Glazed pinwheel poles with multiple flowers, 1-3/8" d. *Collection of Auction Block.*

III-180. Glazed pinwheel poles with multiple flowers, 1-3/8" d. Reverse of #179. *Collection of Auction Block.*

III-181. Glazed pinwheel poles with multiple flowers, 1-3/8" d. End view of #179. *Collection of Auction Block.*

III-182. Unglazed flower china, 1-1/8" d.

III-183. Unglazed flower china, 1-1/8" d. Reverse of #182.

III-184. Unglazed donut hole flower china, 15/16" d.

III-185. Unglazed donut hole flower china, 15/16" d. Reverse of #184.

III-186. Glazed pinwheel poles with central flowers, 1-5/8" d.

III-187. Glazed pinwheel poles with central roses, 1-1/2" d.

III-188. Glazed pinwheel poles with central roses, 1-1/2" d. Reverse of #187.

III-139. Glazed pinwheel poles with central roses, 1-1/2" d. *Collection of Bill Sweet.*

III-190. Glazed pinwheel poles with central roses, 1-1/2" d. Reverse of #189. *Collection of Bill Sweet.*

III-191. Glazed double king's roses. 1-1/8" d. *Collection of Bill Sweet.*

III-192. Glazed double king's roses, 1-1/8" d. Side view of #191. *Collection of Bill Sweet.*

III-193. Unglazed donut flower, 1-1/4" d. *Collection of Wayne Sanders.*

III-194. Glazed five petal flower, 7/8" d. *Collection of Wayne Sanders.*

III-195. Glazed three petal orange flower, 3/4" d. *Collection of Peter Sharrer.*

III-196. Glazed china vines and roses, 7/8" d. *Collection of Jerry Biern.*

III-197. Unglazed five petal flower, 7/8" d. *Collection of Peter Sharrer.*

III-198. Unglazed five petal flower, 7/8" d. Side view of #197. *Collection of Peter Sharrer.*

III-199. Unglazed five petal flower, 7/8" d. Reverse of #197. *Collection of Peter Sharrer.*

III-200. Glazed five petal flower, 7/8" d. *Collection of Jeff Yale.*

III-201. Glazed five petal flower, 7/8" d. Side view of #200. *Collection of Jeff Yale.*

III-202. Unglazed pinwheel poles with vines and flowers, 7/8" d. *Collection of Peter Sharrer.*

III-203. Unglazed pinwheel poles with vines and flowers, 7/8" d. End view of #202. *Collection of Peter Sharrer.*

III-204. Unglazed spiral china, 1-7/8" d. *Collection of Bob Pommrehn.*

III-205. Unglazed spiral china, 1-7/8" d. Side view of #204. *Collection of Bob Pommrehn.*

III-206. Unglazed spiral china, 1-1/2" d. *Collection of Wayne Sanders.*

III-207. Unglazed spiral china, 1-1/2" d. Side view of #206. *Collection of Wayne Sanders.*

III-208. Unglazed helix with leaves, 1-3/16" d. Side view.

III-209 Unglazed helix with leaves, 1-3/16" d. End view of #208.

III-210. Glazed helix china, 1/2" d.

III-211. Glazed helix china, 1/2" d. End view of #210.

III-212. Glazed starburst china, 1-1/4" d. *Collection of Wayne Sanders.*

III-213. Glazed pinwheel china, 1-3/16" d. Side view.

III-214. Glazed pinwheel china, 1-3/16" d. End view of #213.

III-215. Unglazed starburst china, 11/16" d.

III-216. Unglazed pinwheel china, 1" d.

III-217. Unglazed pinwheel china, 1" d. Reverse end of #216.

III-218. Unglazed pinwheel china, 1" d. Side view of #216.

III-219. Unglazed quadrant china with leaves, 11/16" d.

III-220. Unglazed quadrant china with leaves, 11/16" d. Reverse end of #219.

III-221. Unglazed pinwheel china, 3/4" d.

III-222. Unglazed pinwheel china, 3/4" d. Side view of #221.

III-223. Unglazed pinwheel style china, 11/16" d. Side view.

III-224. Unglazed pinwheel style china, 11/16" d. End view of #223.

III-225. Unglazed pinwheel style china, 3/4" d. End view.

III-226. Glazed pinwheel style china, 3/4" d. Side view. *Collection of Jerry Biern.*

III-227. Glazed starburst style china, 1-1/2" d.

III-228. Glazed starburst style china, 1-1/2" d. Side view.

III-229. Glazed pinwheel china, 15/16" d.

III-230. Glazed pinwheel china, 15/16" d. Side view of #229.

III-231. Glazed starburst china, 1-1/4" d. *Collection of Wayne Sanders.*

III-232. Glazed starburst china, 7/8" d. *Collection of Hansel DeSousa.*

III-235. Glazed starburst china, 1-1/4" d. *Collection of Jeff Yale.*

III-233. Unglazed starburst china, 13/16" d. *Collection of Jerry Biern.*

III-236. Glazed starburst china, 7/8" d. *Collection of Jeff Yale.*

III-234. Unglazed starburst china, 13/16" d. Reverse of #233. *Collection of Jerry Biern.*

III-237. Glazed starburst china, 7/8" d. Side view of #236. *Collection of Jeff Yale.*

III-238. Glazed leaf china, 1" d. *Collection of Jeff Yale.*

III-239. Unglazed starburst china, 3/4" d. *Collection of Jerry Biern.*

III-240. Pennsylvania Dutch style, 1-3/8" d. *Collection of Jerry Biern.*

III-241. Pennsylvania Dutch style, 1-3/8" d. Side view of #240. *Collection of Jerry Biern.*

III-242. Pennsylvania Dutch style, 1-3/4" d. *Collection of Jerry Biern.*

III-243. Pennsylvania Dutch style, 1-3/4" d. Side view of #242. *Collection of Jerry Biern.*

III-244. Pennsylvania Dutch style, 1-3/8" d. Side view. *Collection of Jerry Biern.*

III-245 Pennsylvania Dutch style, 1-3/8" d. End view of #244. *Collection of Jerry Biern.*

III-246. Pennsylvania Dutch style, 1-1/2" d. Side view.

III-247. Pennsylvania Dutch style, 1-1/2" d. End view of #246.

III-248. Pennsylvania Dutch style, 1-1/2" d. *Collection of Jeff Yale.*

III-249. Pennsylvania Dutch style, 1-3/8" d. *Collection of Jeff Yale.*

III-250. Pennsylvania Dutch style, 1-1/2" d. End view. *Collection of Jeff Yale.*

III-251. Pennsylvania Dutch style, 1-1/2" d. Side view of #250. *Collection of Jeff Yale.*

III-252. Pennsylvania Dutch style, 1-1/2" d. End view. *Collection of Jeff Yale.*

III-253. Pennsylvania Dutch style, 1-1/2" d. Side view of #252. *Collection of Jeff Yale.*

III-254. Pennsylvania Dutch style, 1-1/2" d. End view. *Collection of Jeff Yale.*

III-255. Pennsylvania Dutch style, 1-1/2" d. Side view of #254. *Collection of Jeff Yale.*

III-256. Scenic china with pinwheel poles, 1-1/4" d. *Collection of Hansel DeSousa.*

III-257. Scenic china with pinwheel poles, 1-3/8" d. *Collection of Hansel DeSousa.*

III-258. Scenic china with pinwheel poles, 1-1/2" d. *Collection of Hansel DeSousa.*

III-259. Scenic china with pinwheel poles, 1-1/2" d. *Collection of Hansel DeSousa.*

III-260. Scenic china with pinwheel poles, 1-3/8" d. *Collection of Hansel DeSousa.*

III-261. Scenic china with pinwheel poles, 1-3/8" d. Reverse of #260. *Collection of Hansel DeSousa.*

III-262. Scenic china with pinwheel poles, 1-3/8" d.

III-263. Scenic china with pinwheel poles, 1-3/8" d. Reverse of #262.

III-264. Scenic china, cane handle type, 1-3/8" d.

III-265. Scenic china, cane handle type, 1-1/2" d.

III-266. Scenic china, cane handle type. Top view of #265.

III-267. Scenic china, cane handle type, 1-3/8" d. *Anonymous.*

III-268. Scenic china, cane handle type, 1-1/2" d. *Anonymous.*

III-269. Scenic china, cane handle type, 1-3/8" d. *Collection of Nancy Zeloski.*

III-270. Scenic china, cane handle type, 1-3/8" d. *Collection of Nancy Zeloski.*

III-271. Scenic china, cane handle type, 1-3/8" d. Side view of #270. *Collection of Nancy Zeloski.*

III-272. Unglazed phoenix and fleur de lis, 13/16" d. *Collection of Jerry Biern.*

III-273. Unglazed eagle and fleur de lis, 13/16" d. *Collection of Jerry Biern.*

III-274. Unglazed ibis, 3/4" d.
Collection of Jerry Biern.

III-275. Unglazed phoenix, 3/4" d.
Collection of Jerry Biern.

III-276. Unglazed phoenix, 3/4" d. Side view of #275. *Collection of Jerry Biern.*

III-277. Glazed china with whales, 1-3/8" d.

III-278. Group of checkerboard Chinas.

III-279. Glazed checkerboard china, 3/4" d

III-280. Glazed checkerboard china, 3/4" d. Reverse of #279.

III-281. Unglazed checkerboard china, 23/32" d.

III-282. Unglazed checkerboard china, 22/32" d. Reverse of #281.

III-283. Unglazed checkerboard china, 11/16" d.

III-284. Unglazed checkerboard china, 3/4" d.

III-285. Unglazed checkerboard china, 3/4" d Reverse end of #284.

III-286. Glazed checkerboard china, 13/16" d. *Collection of Jerry Biern.*

III-287. Glazed checkerboard china, 13/16" d. Reverse of #286. *Collection of Jerry Biern.*

III-288. Carpet ball, 2-7/8" d. *Collection of Jeff Yale.*

III-289. Carpet ball, 2-7/8" d.

III-290. Carpet ball, 2-7/8" d. *Collection of Jeff Yale.*

III-291. Carpet ball, 2-7/8" d. *Collection of Jeff Yale.*

III-292. Carpet ball, 2-7/8" d. *Collection of Jeff Yale.*

III-293. Carpet ball, 2-1/4" d.

III-294. Carpet ball, 2-1/2" d.

III-295. Carpet ball, 2-1/2" d. Reverse of #294.

III-296. Carpet ball, 2-1/8" d.

III-297. Carpet ball, 2-1/8" d. Reverse of #296.

III-298. Carpet ball, 2-7/8" d.

III-299. Carpet ball, 2-1/2" d.

III-300. Carpet ball, 2-1/2" d.
Collection of Jeff Yale.

III-301. Carpet ball, 2-1/2" d. End view.

III-302. Carpet ball, 2-1/2" d. Side view of #301.

III-303. Carpet ball, 2-3/4" d.
Collection of Jeff Yale.

III-304. Carpet ball, 2-1/4" d.

III-305. Carpet ball, 2-1/4" d. Reverse of #304.

III-306. Carpet ball, 2-1/2" d.

III-307. Carpet ball, 2-1/4" d.

III-308. Carpet ball, 2-1/2" d.
Collection of Jeff Yale.

III-309. Carpet ball, 2-1/2" d.
Collection of Jeff Yale.

III-310. Carpet ball, 2-1/2" d.
Collection of Auction Blocks.

III-311. Contemporary carpet ball, 1-3/4" d.

III-312. Contemporary carpet ball, 1-3/4" d.

III-313. Contemporary carpet ball, 1-1/2" d.

III-314. Contemporary lined china, 1-3/8" d.

III-315. Contemporary lined china, 1-3/8" d. Reverse of #314.

III-316. Contemporary lined china, 1-3/8" d.

III-317. Contemporary lined china, 1-3/4" d. *Collection of Mark Block.*

III-318. Contemporary lined china, 1-3/4" d. Reverse of #317. *Collection of Mark Block.*

III-319. Contemporary lined china, 1" d. *Collection of Mark Block.*

III-320. Contemporary checkerboard china, 2-1/8" d. *Collection of Mark Block.*

III-321. Contemporary checkerboard china, 1-1/4" d. *Collection of Mark Block.*

III-322. Contemporary lined china, 1-1/4" d. *Collection of Mark Block.*

III-323. Contemporary decorated china, 1-1/4" d. *Collection of Mark Block.*

III-324. Contemporary decorated china, 1-1/4" d. Side view of #323. *Collection of Mark Block.*

III-325. Contemporary flower china, 1-1/8" d.

III-326. Contemporary flower china, 1-1/8" d. Side view of #325.

III-327. Contemporary flower china, 2" d. *Collection of Mark Block.*

III-328. Contemporary flower china, 2" d. Side view of #327. *Collection of Mark Block.*

III-329. Contemporary flower china, 2" d. End view of #327. *Collection of Mark Block.*

III-330. Contemporary scenic china, 1-1/2" d. *Collection of Mark Block.*

III-331. Contemporary scenic china, 1-1/8" d. *Collection of Mark Block.*

III-332. Contemporary flower china, 1-1/8" d. *Collection of Mark Block.*

III-333. Contemporary flower china, 1-1/8" d. Side view of #332. *Collection of Mark Block.*

III-334. Contemporary fruit china, 1" d. *Collection of Mark Block.*

III-335. Contemporary fruit china, 1" d. Side view of #334. *Collection of Mark Block*

III-336. Contemporary Pennsylvania Dutch style china, 1" d. *Collection of Mark Block*

III-337. Contemporary Pennsylvania Dutch style china, 1" d. Side view of #336. *Collection of Mark Block*

III-338. Contemporary millefiori china, 1-3/8" d. *Collection of Mark Block.*

III-339. Contemporary decorated china, 1-3/8" d. *Collection of Mark Block.*

III-340. Contemporary decorated china, 1-3/8" d. *Collection of Mark Block.*

III-341. Contemporary decorated china, 1-3/8" d.

III-342. Contemporary decorated china, 1-3/8" d. Reverse of #341.

III-343. Contemporary scenic china, 1-1/4" d. *Collection of Mark Block.*

III-344. Contemporary scenic china, 1-1/4" d. Top view of #343. *Collection of Mark Block.*

III-345. Contemporary scenic china, 1-1/2" d. Top view. *Collection of Mark Block.*

III-346. Contemporary scenic china, 1-1/2" d. Side view of #345. *Collection of Mark Block.*

III-347. Contemporary scenic china, 1-1/2" d. Reverse side of #345. *Collection of Mark Block.*

III-348. Contemporary scenic china, 1-1/2" d. Top view. *Collection of Mark Block.*

III-349. Contemporary scenic china, 1-1/2" d. Bottom view of #348. *Collection of Mark Block.*

III-350. Contemporary decorated china, 1-1/4" d. Top view. *Collection of Mark Block.*

III-351. Contemporary decorated china, 1-1/4" d. Side view of #350. *Collection of Mark Block.*

III-352. Contemporary decorated china, 2" d. *Collection of Nadine MacDonald.*

III-353. Contemporary decorated china, 1-1/2" d. *Collection of Mark Block.*

III-354. Contemporary decorated china, 1-1/2" d. Reverse side of #353. *Collection of Mark Block.*

III-355 Contemporary decorated china, 1-1/2" d. Top view. *Collection of Mark Block.*

III-356. Contemporary decorated china, 1-1/2" d. Side view of #355. *Collection of Mark Block.*

III-357. Contemporary decorated china, 1-1/2" d. *Collection of Mark Block.*

III-358. Contemporary decorated china, 1-1/2" d. Side view of #357. *Collection of Mark Block.*

III-359. Contemporary scenic china, 1-1/4" d. *Collection of Mark Block.*

III-360. Contemporary scenic china, 1-1/4" d. Reverse of #359. *Collection of Mark Block.*

III-361. Game board and decorated Chinas, 7" d. board, 3/4" d. marbles. *Collection of Nadine MacDonald.*

Section IV: Other Materials

Marbles have been produced with any material that can be fashioned to a round ball. Some of the materials used are too soft to stand the rigors of play and are used primarily for decorative purposes. Others were too hard and would damage marbles of other materials. These were usually banned by the other players. Examples of the latter type are ball bearings and, to a lesser degree, Agate marbles. They would destroy marbles made of clay, china, porcelain, pottery, and glass while sustaining little or no damage. Many players, including the author, would have a prize agate shooter to use, however, as often as not, they weren't allowed in the game. If the opponents in the game had their own prized shooters, then pride and competitiveness allowed the games to continue.

This section covers various other materials used for marbles. For reference purposes, it is divided into two groupings: materials used before 1960 and modern materials used for marbles after 1960.

Marbles from the earlier period include cloisonné, gutta-percha, metal, paper mache, scrimshaw, and wood.

Cloisonné is enamelware in which the decoration is formed by different colors of enamel, separated by thin strips of metal set on edge. With marbles, these are usually hollow balls not meant to be played with, as they are very fragile. Very few early examples exist. They were probably originally made to be cane or parasol handles, or light pulls. Sizes usually are over 1" in diameter. They rarely come up for sale. Therefore, an accurate valuation for this type is difficult to ascertain.

Gutta-percha is a hard rubbery substance from the latex (sap) of certain tropical trees. The substance forms a hard plastic-like material (see photo numbers IV 39 through IV 57).

Valuation	Mint	Near Mint
3/4" - 7/8"	$200-350	$50-100
1" and over	$350-700	$75-200

Metal — Metal formed into a ball. Solid metal balls are usually ball bearings. The collectible marble type are hollow steel balls that were made to be marbles. They have crossed slits at one end (+) where the formed metal ball was closed.

Valuation	Mint	Near Mint
to 3/4" d.	$15-25	$5-10
7/8" and over	$40-200	$15-50

Paper Mache — Marbles made from paper pulp or paper fibers mixed with glue or paste that become hard when dry and are then suitable for painting and decorating. The base material may also be mascerated money.

Valuation	Mint	Near Mint
3/4" - 7/8" d.	$75-150	$15-50
1" and over	$200-400	$50-100

Scrimshaw — Bone fashioned into marbles then decorated with etchings or carvings. Few original examples exist therefore valuations are difficult.

Valuation	Mint	Near Mint
over 1" d.	$300-1,500	$100-500

The more intricate and elaborate the carving, the more valuable the marble.

Wood — May be natural, dyed or handpainted.

Valuation	Mint	Near Mint
Natural or Dyed (any size)	$.10-25	$.05-1
Handpainted Decoration (any size)	$5-25	$.50-3

More recent marbles have been made of cement and fiber optics.

Cement — Marbles have been made by powdered, calcined rock and clay materials that form a paste when wet. They can then be molded, extruded, and formed into a solid mass suitable for hand painting (see photo numbers IV 1 through IV 9).

Valuation: Few have come on the market, therefore valuation is difficult. Nice examples have been made on a limited personal craft basis. Pricing would be similar to those of contemporary potteries and chinas.

Fiber Optics — Are a formulation of glass fibers and resins, forming a very hard material (see photo numbers IV 12 through IV 38).

Valuation	Mint
3/4" - 7/8"	$5-10

1" and over	$15-25	

Plastics — Are made of complex organic compounds produced by polymerization. The resultant material can be formed by molding, extruding or casting. They may be clear or opaque (see photo numbers IV 64 through IV 72). There is also a plastic material that has the look of scrimshaw. Modern game boards have been made with this type of material.

Valuation	**Mint**	**Near Mint**
any size	$.50-4	$.10-.50
Contemporary Scrimshaw Types		
over 1" d.	$10-100	$5-20

In addition to the above mentioned varieties, it should be noted that some of the marbles produced by modern craftsmen may contain a combination of materials such as clays, plastics, and glass. This relatively new experimentation is in its infancy and may produce some very interesting results. Time will tell.

IV-1. Modern hand-painted unglazed cement, 2-1/16" d.

IV-2. Modern hand-painted unglazed cement, 2-1/16" d. Top view of #1.

IV-3. Modern hand-painted unglazed cement, 2-1/16" d. Bottom view of #1.

IV-4. Modern hand-painted unglazed cement, 2-1/16" d.

IV-5. Modern hand-painted unglazed cement, 2-1/16" d. Top view of #4.

IV-6. Modern hand-painted glazed cement, 2-1/4" d.

IV-7. Modern hand-painted glazed cement, 2" d.

IV-8. Modern hand-painted glazed cement, 1-3/4" d.

IV-9. Modern hand-painted glazed cement, 1-3/4" d. Reverse of #8.

IV-10. Modern cloisonné marble, 1-3/8" d.

IV-11. Group of fiber optic marbles.

IV-12. Fiber optic marble, 3/4" d.

IV-13. Fiber optic marble, 3/4" d.
Reverse of #12.

IV-14. Fiber optic marble, 11/16" d.

IV-15. Fiber optic marble, 11/16" d.
Reverse of #14.

IV-16. Fiber optic marble, 3/4" d.

IV-17. Fiber optic marble, 11/16" d.

IV-18. Fiber optic marble, 11/16" d.
Reverse of #17.

IV-19. Fiber optic marble, 3/4" d.

IV-20. Fiber optic marble, 3/4" d.

IV-21. Fiber optic marble, 11/16" d.

IV-22. Fiber optic marble, 11/16" d. Reverse of #21.

IV-23. Fiber optic marble, 11/16" d.

IV-24. Fiber optic marble, 11/16" d. Reverse of #23.

IV-25. Tri-color fiber optic marble, 11/16" d.

IV-26. Tri-color fiber optic marble, 11/16" d. Side view of #25.

IV-27. Tri-color fiber optic marble, 11/16" d. Reverse of #26.

IV-28. Fiber optic marble, 11/16" d.

IV-29. Fiber optic marble, 11/16" d. End view of #28.

IV-30. Fiber optic marble, 3/4" d.

IV-31. Fiber optic marble, 11/16" d.

IV-32. Fiber optic marble, 11/16" d. Reverse of #31.

IV-33. Fiber optic marble, 11/16" d. End view of #31.

IV-34. Fiber optic marble, 3/4" d.

IV-35. Tri-color fiber optic marble, 1-1/2" d. *Collection of Nadine MacDonald.*

IV-36. Fiber optic marble, 1" d. *Collection of Nadine MacDonald.*

IV-37. Fiber optic marble, 1" d. *Collection of Nadine MacDonald.*

IV-38. Fiber optic marble, 1" d. *Collection of Nadine MacDonald.*

IV-39. Gutta-percha group photo. *Collection of Robert Block.*

IV-40. Gutta-percha, 13/16" d.
Collection of Robert Block.

IV-41. Gutta-percha, 13/16" d.
Collection of Robert Block.

IV-42. Gutta-percha, 1" d.
Collection of Robert Block.

IV-43. Gutta-percha, 1" d. Reverse of #42.
Collection of Robert Block.

IV-44. Gutta-percha, 1" d.
Collection of Robert Block.

IV-45. Gutta-percha, 7/8" d.
Collection of Robert Block.

IV-46. Gutta-percha, 1" d. *Collection of Robert Block.*

IV-47. Gutta-percha, 15/16" d. *Collection of Robert Block.*

IV-48. Gutta-percha, 7/8" d. *Collection of Robert Block.*

IV-49. Gutta-percha, 7/8" d. *Collection of Robert Block.*

IV-50. Gutta-percha, 1" d. *Collection of Robert Block.*

IV-51. Gutta-percha, 1" d. *Collection of Robert Block.*

IV-52. Gutta-percha, 15/16" d. *Collection of Robert Block.*

IV-53. Gutta-percha, 15/16" d. *Collection of Robert Block.*

IV-54. Gutta-percha, 13/16" d. *Collection of Robert Block.*

IV-55. Gutta-percha, 1" d. *Collection of Robert Block.*

IV-56. Gutta-percha, 1" d. *Collection of Robert Block.*

IV-57. Gutta-percha, 1" d. *Collection of Robert Block.*

IV-58. Paper mache, 1-1/8" d. *Collection of Bill Sweet.*

IV-59. Paper mache, 1-1/8" d. End view of #58. *Collection of Bill Sweet.*

IV-60. Paper mache, 1-1/8" d. Side view of #58. *Collection of Bill Sweet.*

IV-61. Paper mache, 15/16" d. *Collection of Robert Block.*

IV-62. Paper mache, 15/16" d. Reverse of #61. *Collectior of Robert Block.*

IV-63. Paper mache, 15/16" d. End view of #61. *Collection of Robert Block.*

IV-64. Plastic, 1-1/8" d. *Collection of David Terrell.*

IV-65. Plastic, 1-1/8" d. Reverse of #64. *Collection of David Terrell.*

IV-66. Plastic, 1-1/8" d. *Collection of David Terrell.*

IV-67. Plastic, 3/4" d. *Collection of David Terrell.*

IV-68. Plastic, 1" d. *Collection of Robert Block.*

IV-69. Plastic, 1" d. Reverse of #68. *Collection of Robert Block.*

IV-70. Plastic, 3/4" d. *Collection of Robert Block.*

IV-71. Plastic, 3/4" d. Reverse of #70. *Collection of Robert Block.*

IV-72. Plastic, 11/16" d.

IV-73. Scrimshaw, 1-3/4" d.

IV-74. Scrimshaw, 1-3/4" d. Side view of #73.

IV-75. Scrimshaw, 1-3/4" d. Reverse of #74.

IV-76. Scrimshaw, 1-3/4" d.

IV-77. Scrimshaw, 1-3/4" d. Upside down view of #76.

IV-78. Scrimshaw, 1-3/4" d.

IV-79. Scrimshaw, 1-3/4" d.

IV-80. Scrimshaw, 1-3/4" d. Reverse of #79.

IV-81. Scrimshaw, 1-3/4" d. Top view of #79.

IV-82. Scrimshaw, 1-3/4" d. Side view of #79.

IV-83. Hollow Steelie, 1" d.

IV-84. Hand-painted wood, 1-1/4" d. *Collection of Les Jones.*

IV-85. Hand-painted wood, 1-1/4" d. Side and bottom view. *Collection of Les Jones*

Glossary of Terms

This glossary of terms presents accepted definitions of marbles and related terms.

AGATE. (1) Any marble made of agate, either handmade or machine-made. Genuine antique handmade agate marbles are identified by the many minute facets that are the result of hand grinding. (2) A variegated stone, chalcedony, having its colors arranged in bands or stripes, blended in clouds, or showing moss-like forms. Most shades of earth colors occur, but the most common are alterations of reddish-browns with white. Agate can be dyed. *See also* CHALCEDONY.

AGATE MARBLES. Marbles ground from agate, and historically prized for their durability and beauty. Also called carnelians. *See also* AGATE.

AGGIES. A common term used on the playgrounds of earlier times to refer to both glass and stone playing marbles of better quality or favored sort.

ALLEYS. Derived from alleytors; prized shooters made of semi-precious minerals. *See also* AGGIES.

ANNEAL. The process of gradually reducing glass temperatures, usually in an oven or lehr, for the purpose of balancing internal stresses throughout the glass, resulting in the prevention of fractures when the object reaches room temperature.

ANTIQUE. According to United States customs laws: an item, usually a work of art, furniture, or decorative object made at least one hundred years ago.

AVENTURINE. (1) Type of glass containing small particles of either copper (goldstone), chromic oxide (green aventurine) or ferric oxide (red aventurine), giving glass an intensely glittering appearance (*see also* LUTZ).

BATCH. Mixture of raw materials, properly proportioned and mixed, ready for use in the manufacture of glass. Typical mixture includes: (1) silica sand (the relatively pure quartz base material); (2) soda or potash to lower the melting point; (3) lime to harden and make the metal easier to work; (4) lead for brilliance; (5) borax for greater hardness; (6) metallic oxides to clear and color; and (7) cullet to lower the melting temperature of the batch.

BENNINGTONS. Glazed pottery (crockery) marble, most often found in blues, browns, greens, and mottled colors. *See also* CLAY, POTTERY.

BLOODSTONE. Green chalcedony highlighted by red spots that resemble blood, and results from the oxidizing of the green material. Also known as heliotrope, it is considered a semiprecious stone. *See also* CHALCEDONY.

BOWLS. Also known as carpet balls (bowls). Stone, porcelain or pottery spheres in various colors or patterns. About 3 inches in diameter, they are used in lawn, or small scale indoor bowling games. *See also* BOWLING.

BOWLING. (1) Rolling the shot on the ground to hit a marble; (2) any of several games in which balls are rolled on an outdoor green, or down an indoor alley, at an object or group of objects.

BRUISED. The CONDITION of a marble that has received a visibly damaging blow, but no part has been chipped off. Sometimes bruising does not reduce the value quite as much as chips. *See also* CONDITION.

BULL'S-EYE. (1) China marbles with concentric rings forming target design. (2) Agate marbles with the same "eye" design.

BUMBOOZER. A very large marble (1 inch and over) used as a bowling shooter. *See also* HOGGER.

CALCAREOUS. Stone having the nature of calcite or calcium carbonate, especially in hardness. For example, limestone and chalcedony.

CALCITE. A mineral formed of calcium carbonate crystallized in hexagonal form. It cleaves readily into rhombohedrons, and includes variations of chalk, limestone, dogtooth spar, Iceland spar, stalactites, stalagmites, and marble among others.

CARNELIAN. (1) Colloquially, a marble made of agate. (2) A variety of chalcedony of a deep-red, flesh-red, or reddish-white color. Considered a semiprecious stone. *See also* AGATE, CHALCEDONY, and QUARTZ.

CARPET BOWLS (BALLS). *See* BOWLS.

CERAMICS. Any of various hard, brittle, heat resistant, and corrosion resistant materials made by firing clay or other minerals.

CHALCEDONY. A translucent to opaque variety of quartz, most commonly pale tints of blue or gray, and wax-like luster. A semi-precious stone. Chalcedony of special or variegated colors is known as carnelian, agate, onyx, etc.

CHALKIES. Unglazed marbles made of gypsum, sometimes clay or limestone.

CHASIES. Marble game, usually with two players. Players alternate shooting at each other's marble. Also known as "follow-up" (Midwest).

CHINAS. Marbles made of porcelain. May be glazed or unglazed. Most often decorated with concentric rings of different colors, others are painted with flowers, fruit, trees, and other motif. Also called chinee, or chiny on the playground. *See also* PORCELAIN and POTTERY.

CHIPS. Pieces broken from the surface of a marble.

CLAYS. Marbles made of clay that may or may not be colored or glazed. Common clays can be referred to as Commonys, or Commies.

CLOISSONE. Colored decoration of enamels poured into areas divided by wire or metal strips.

CLOUDY. Lacking clearness, brightness, or luster. When caused by surface wear it reduces the value and quality of the marble. *See also* CONDITION.

COLLECTIBLE. The worst marble condition expected in a collection. Badly damaged, but has some redeeming features. *See also* CONDITION.

COLLECTOR. One who gathers specimens for the purpose of study or ornament. Contrasts with accumulator in implying more careful selection that leads to enjoyment of the aesthetic values pursued ... and the knowledge gained and shared in fellowship.

COMICS. Called "picture marbles" by Peltier Glass Co. when produced from 1926 through the early 1930s. Twelve comic-strip character faces and names (Annie, Betty, Sandy, Ko Ko, Moon, Skeezix, Bimbo, Emma, Kayo, Smitty, Andy, Herbie) were printed on the marbles by a patented process that included a clear overglaze for permanence of the images.

CONDITION AND GRADING. The grading of condition is very subjective. Every collector has their own opinion and no two collectors will likely agree on the exact condition of a particular marble. The Marble Collectors Society of America uses a descriptive grading system (Mint, Near Mint, Good, Collectible), which allows for some flexibility in grading. A numerical grading system based on a scale of 1 to 10 has also developed among marble collectors. The descriptions of each grading label used by the Society, along with the equivalent numerical grading is:

Mint: A marble that is in original condition. The surface is unmarked and undamaged. There may be some minor rubbing on the surface, however, the marble is just the way it came from the factory. (10.0 - 9.0)

Near Mint: A marble that has experienced minor usage. There may be evidence of some hit marks, usually tiny subsurface moons, pinprick chips, tiny flakes, or tiny bruises. The damage is inconsequential and does not detract from viewing the marble. If there is noticeable damage, and it is on only one side of the marble, the other side is considered Mint. (8.9 - 8.0)

Good: A marble that has experienced minor usage. It will have numerous hit marks, subsurface moons, chips, flakes, or bruises. The core can still be clearly seen, but the marble shows obvious use. If the damage is large or deep, and it is confined to one side the other side is considered Mint to Near Mint. (7.9 - 7.0)

Collectible: A marble that has experienced significant usage. Overall moons, chips, flakes, and bruises. The core is completely obscured in some spots. A collectible marble has served its purpose and been well used. Still, it is a placeholder in a collection until a better example replaces it. (6.9 - 0.0)

Any damage to the surface of a marble, no matter how slight, will affect its value. For a given amount of damage, the depreciation of value is much greater for machine-made marbles than for handmade marbles. Even a small chip will effectively reduce the value of a machine-made marble by more than half. Collectors tend to be more forgiving of damage to a handmade marble; this is likely because handmade marbles are more difficult to find.

The size of a marble is generally measured by its diameter in inches. Marble manufacturers utilize a sieve system of measuring. Using a device that measured marbles in 1/16-inch increments, the smallest opening that the marble would fall through was its size. Because of this method, the marbles classified as one size by a manufacturer could in fact vary by 3/64 inch. It was technically impossible to produce antique handmade glass marbles in sizes greater than approximately 2-1/2 inches in diameter because such marbles would sag and deform during the annealing process due to the weight. However, different types of marbles are more common in some sizes than others. Machine-made marbles are usually 1/2 inch to 3/4 inch. This is because marble tournament regulations set the size of the shooters to be between 1/2 inch and 3/4 inch and the size of the target marbles to be 5/8 inch. Again, the relative rarity of different sizes varies greatly from one type of marble to another.

CRAZING. A network of fine cracks in the surface of a marble that can be caused by improper glazing of clays or annealing of glass.

CROCKIES. Clay marbles in either solid or mottled colors, often glazed earthenware.

DIAMETER. The length of a straight line through the center of an object. The size of a marble is measured by its greatest diameter.

DING. Minor damage to a marble caused by a blow, resulting in a small chip missing.

DOBIES. A term referring to clay or common marbles.

DOUGH BABY. A clay marble term (of California origin); possibly a variation of "adobe," a clay for bricks.

DUBS. Knocking two or more marbles out of the ring with one shot.

EXCELLENT. An obscure term when referring to condition of a marble. Mint is less subjective, and has been recognized to describe the best condition of a marble that remains undamaged but not in its original container. *See also* MINT, CONDITION.

FEN. Used as a ritual call by children, especially in certain games (as marbles) to prevent certain actions by an opponent or teammate, or to exempt the first caller from a task or action. Meant to prevent (e.g., fen cubs) a player, upon hitting two marbles in one shot, from taking both.

FIBER OPTIC. Transparent fibers of glass or plastic fused together.

FLINT. (1) A somewhat impure quartz that ranges in color from light gray to brown-black. Handmade flint marbles do exist. (2) Crystal glass, so called because a fine antique British glass was originally made by substituting pulverized flint for silica sand. *See also* BATCH.

FOR FAIR. Playing so as to return to the former owner all marbles won during the game.

FOR KEEPS. Playing without returning opponent's marbles.

FUDGING. Easing the hand over ring line when in the act of shooting. Forbidden in tournament play. Term replaces "cheating" if opponent is a big kid.

GENERAL GRANT GAME BOARD. An early form of the board game "Solitaire." This game board was round and had a hand-painted silhouette of the bust of Grant on the surface of the board.

GLAZE. The vitreous (glass) coating on china and pottery marbles that imparts the smooth glossy finish. Applied as either liquid or powder (flour glaze), the marbles are again heated and ANNEALED. Dull pottery marbles are unglazed, or glaze has lost its sheen through use or abuse. COMICS received a flour glaze after the picture was applied. *See also* COMICS

GOOD. Third from best CONDITION on a scale of four. *See also* CONDITION.

GRANITE. Marbles made of granite, a hard igneous rock that takes a high polish.

GUTTA-PERCHA. A rubbery substance from the latex of several tropical trees.

HANDMADE. Marbles made without use of machines, the exception being those held in the fingers against a power driven grinding wheel (e.g., agates made before 1910). Few handmade marbles of any sort can be expected to be perfect spheres; clay, pottery, and china types are most out-of-round.

HISTING. Raising the hand from the ground while in the act of shooting. Not allowed in tournament play. The cause of many blackened eyes.

HOGGER. Any marble larger than 7/8 inch, and typically approximately 1 inch. Commonly, and misleadingly, called "shooter" size. Very few marbles were won with one of those big targets, and are nearly impossible to shoot properly off the knuckle.

HUNCHING. Moving the hand forward while shooting over the ring line. Not allowed in tournament play. Also known as poling (Midwest).

JADES. Marbles made of the gemstone jade, usually green.

JASPERS. (1) Marbles made of jasper, a form of CHALCEDONY. (2) Playground name for LINED CROCKERY marbles.

KABOLA. Oversized marble of jawbreaker size. *See also* HOGGER.

KLICKERS. Old name for marbles made of agate and semiprecious stone, mentioned by Paul Baumann in *Collecting Antique Marbles*, and still currently in use in Europe.

KNUCKLES DOWN. To rest one or more of one's knuckles on the ground while shooting. A general term denoting the correct form for marble shooting. The marble should rest against the ball of the first finger rather than in the crook.

LAG. To pitch or shoot at a mark, marble, hole or other target. In some areas (Midwest) to pitch as distinguished from shoot.

LAG LINE. A straight-line tangent to the ring in tournament play.

LAGGING. The act of tossing or shooting from the pitching line. Whoever comes closest to the lag line, without going over it, shoots first.

LINED CROCKERY. A type of pottery marble made from two or more colors of clay, which produce random areas of sharp contrast. Also called JASPERS. *See also* POTTERY.

LOFTING. The act of shooting a marble through the air in an arc to hit another marble, or other target. Sometimes called popping.

LUTZ. A type of glass containing Aventurine.

MARBLES. Marbles are little balls made of hard substances (as stone, glass, porcelain, clay, metal, etc.) typically from 5/8 inch to 2 inches in diameter. Decorative marbles are as large as 3 inches and as small as 1/4 inch.

M.I.B. The acronym for Mint-in-Box refers to original marbles, in their original box, in original condition. *See also* CONDITION, MINT, NEAR MINT.

MIBS. The game of marbles; represents shortening of the word marbles.

MIGGLES. Common playing marble; term usually referred to small clays. Also called Migs.

MINERAL. Solid crystalline substance not of animal or vegetable substances.

MINT. Established by long usage as the standard term meaning the original undamaged condition. *See also* CONDITION.

MOON AGGIES. Marbles made of CARNELIAN. So called because a blow or hit usually produces a moon or crescent shape fracture inward from the surface rather than a chip. When soaked in mineral oil or lard, the moon may become very difficult to detect. *See also* AGATE.

MOSS AGATE. Variety of agate having inclusions of brown, black, or green moss-like shapes. Realistic tree-like inclusions occur. *See also* AGATE.

NEAR-MINT. Refers to condition of a marble. Accepted by usage as next best grade. *See also* CONDITION.

ONYX. (1) Quartz in parallel layers of different colors. *See also* CHALCEDONY. (2) Onyx seems to have been a catchall term in early catalogs offering machine-made glass marbles.

PEE WEE. Refers to a marble with 1/2 inch or smaller maximum diameter.

PITCH LINE. A straight-line tangent to the ring, directly opposite and parallel to the lag line in the game of ringer. *See also* LAG LINE.

POLISHING. Removal of haze from the surface of a marble. When done properly, does not reduce value of the marble, and can greatly increase its beauty. Performed in a way (similar to grinding) where the polishing compound is applied to a cotton buffer.

POOR. Refers to condition of a marble. Marble has serious damage, chips, and/or cloudy surface. *See also* CONDITION.

PORCELAIN. A hard, fine-grained, non-porous, and most often translucent white ceramic ware that consists primarily of kaolin, quartz, and feldspar. It is fired at high temperature, and does not absorb water. *See also* CHINAS.

POTSIES. Name for the game of ringer. Also called Dubs.

POTTERY. Earthenware as distinguished from porcelain, stonewares, brick, and tile. *See also* BENNINGTONS.

QUARTZ. (1) The most common of all solid materials, it is a form of silica (silicon dioxide) having hexagonal crystals. Typically colorless, but naturally occurring in many colors. (2) Quartz-laden sand is the largest ingredient in making glass. *See also* BATCH.

RING TAW (RINGER). A game in which marbles are placed in a ring marked on the ground, and shot at, with player's taw, from the outer edge of the ring. The player knocking the most marbles from the ring is the winner.

ROSE QUARTZ. A rose-red to pink variety of the mineral quartz.

SHOOTER. (1) In play, the marble shot from the hand. Maximum size allowed in tournament play is 3/4 inch. (2) Mechanical device (usually patented) for propelling a marble. *See also* HOGGER.

SIZE. Usually measured with vernier calipers (brass or plastic), handmade marble size is the longest diameter. Machine-made marbles are sized as follows:

7/16 inch	0000
1/2 inch	000
1/16 inch	00
5/8 inch	0
1/16 inch	1
3/4 inch	2
13/16 inch	3
7/8 inch	4
15/16 inch	5
1 inch	6
1-1/16 inch	7
1-1/8 inch	8

SLIP. (1) Misplay when marble falls from the hand. Player shoots over. (2) Player who drops the marble must call "slips" before Opponent calls "no slips" or looses the turn to shoot over (playgrounds in Midwest) (3) The soupy mixture of clay used to cast sulfide figures. *See also* SULFIDES.

SNOOGER. A near miss in a game of marbles.

SOLITAIRE. Popular marble game of the nineteenth century. Played by one player using a round board (General Grant Game Board) incised with thirty-three round depressions, the object of the game is to remove each jumped marble (as in the game of checkers, draughts) so that one marble remains resting in the center spot on the board. *See also* GENERAL GRANT GAME BOARD.

SPANNERS. A shooting distance. The measurement between the tip of the thumb to the tip of the middle finger when stretched apart.

STEELY. (1) A hollow marble made of steel (sometimes brass) that can be identified by light weight and a "+" on one side where the thin metal meets, made in 1-1/16 inch and 5/8 inch sizes. (2) Common name given to ball bearings.

STICK. A shooter's marble (stops) inside the ring after knocking a target marble out of the ring. The player may continue to shoot as long as the shooter sticks inside the ring.

SULFIDES. Ceramic objects cast or molded of china clay and supersilicate of potash for inclusion in marbles, and other glassware. (Also spelled sulphide.)

TAWS. (1) Term derived from alleytor; prized shooter made of semiprecious minerals. (2) Another name for shooter. (3) The line or other agreed upon starting point of a game of marbles (Midwest).

THRIBS. Term refers to three marbles, and usually used in the ritual call "fen thribs," meaning to prevent an opponent who has hit three marbles from taking more than one.

TIGEREYE. A mineral marble, usually brown, with bright reflecting inside sheen bands, which are usually golden, but may be red or purple. The reflection is caused by asbestos fibers naturally enclosed in a base of quartz.

TWOFERS. Marbles originally priced two for one cent. Anything cheap.

WET MINT. Referring to CONDITION of a marble. Wet mint look can be applied to the surface of a marble with a coating of liquid acrylic floor wax. *See also* CONDITION, MINT, POLISHING.

Bibliography

Baumann, Paul. *Collecting Antique Marbles.* Des Moines, Iowa: Krause Publications, Wallace Homestead Book Co., 1991.

Block, Robert. *Marbles Identification and Price Guide 4th Edition.* Atglen, Pennsylvania: Schiffer Publishing Ltd., 2002.

Block, Stanley. "Marbles Playing for Fun and Keeps," *The Encyclopedia of Collectibles Lalique to Marbles.* Time-Life Publications, 1983.

______. *Marble Mania.* The Marble Collectors Society of America. Atglen, Pennsylvania: Schiffer Publishing Ltd., 1998.

Carskadden, Jeff and Richard Garity. "Chinas." *The Muskingum Valley Archaeological Society*, Zanesville, Ohio, 1990.

Grist, Everett. *Big Book of Marbles.* Paducah, Kentucky: Collector Books, 1993.

Watson, Henry D. "Antique Marbles of Stone, Pottery, and Glass." *American Collector*, July 1942.

Webb, Dennis. *Greenberg's Guide to Marbles 2nd Edition.* Waukesha, Wisconsin: Garenberg Publishing Co., 1994.

Appendices

Appendix 1: Marbles on Computer

By now, most have found themselves bombarded with today's technology revolution—news of the Internet, World Wide Web, cyberspace, the Information Superhighway, "going on-line," and "net surfing." For marble collecting, and antiquing in general, use of the Internet and on-line services are growing at a rapid pace. The Internet has provided collectors with a remarkably efficient means of communicating and exchanging information, as well as other previously non-traditional forms of buying and selling. There are a number of ways you can enhance your marble collecting experience by going "on-line."

Discussion Groups

By having conversations through computers with other collectors, you have another avenue to get your questions answered, buy and sell marbles, and find out about shows and auctions, using one of the on-line service "message boards." You can also participate in the Marble Collectors Mailing List and bulletin board at www.marblecollecting.com. There are also small groups on various networks and servers.

The World Wide Web

The World Wide Web is the fastest growing area for on-line collecting. There is a tremendous wealth of information on the "Web," and more is being added each day. The largest and most comprehensive marble related web site is marblecollecting.com. The MCSA's web site is www.marblemania.com; on-line version of the book *Marbles: Identification and Price Guide*, marble game instructions; marble show schedules; listing of marble clubs; auction information and links; Reproduction Alert page, and classified ads. Collectors are creating more marble related web sites seemingly every day. Marblecollecting.com has an up-to-date listing and links to numerous other marble web sites.

Auctions

Aside from buying and selling marbles on the Web through sites like eBay and Yahoo, you can also use the Internet to participate in marble auctions. The Auction Blocks (www.auctionblocks.com) lists catalogs with images on the Internet and accept valid bids via e-mail for their absentee auctions. Ebay is another on line source for marbles. At any given time, there are several thousand lots of marbles for sale on Ebay.

So, whether you want to connect with other marble collectors, locate information on marbles and marble collectors, or buy and sell marbles, "cyberspace" has fast become an essential element in your collecting repertoire.

When searching the internet for marbles or marble-related items, simply use your favorite search engine, whether it be Google, Yahoo, or another. Simply type in "marbles" and you'll be amazed at the seemingly endless number of marble related web sites that appear.

Appendix II: Marble Clubs

The following is a current listing of marble clubs.

Akro Agate Collector's Club
Roger Hardy
10 Bailey Street
Clarksburg, WV 26301

Badger Marble Club
Jim Stephenson
P.O. Box 194
Waunakee, WI 53597
Show

Buckeye Marble Collectors
Brenda Longbrake
P.O. Box 3051
Elida, OH 45807
Shows, newsletter

Canadian Marble Collectors Association
59 Mill Street
Milton, Ontario, Canada L9T JR8
Newsletters

Great Plains Marble Club
c/o Steve Campbell
508 Sixth Street
Glenwood, IA 51534
Show

Indiana Marble Club
Beth Morris
4803 Ridge Road
Kokomo, IN 46901
(765) 457-2477
Show

International Association of Marble Collectors
Lee Linne
30839 50th Place, S.W.
Federal Way, WA 98023

Kansas City Marble Collectors Club
Craig Snider
(913) 268-9616
www.kcmarbleclub.com

Knuckledown Marble Club
Daniel Ambrose
3112 Amherst Road
Erie, PA 16506

Maine Marble Club
Micki Pasanen
47 Burnham Road
Gorham, ME 04038
Show

Marble Collectors Society of America
Stanley Block
P.O. Box 222
Trumbull, CT 06611
Newsletter, books, videos, other publications

Marble Collectors Unlimited
Gary Huxford
503 W. Pine
Marengo, IA 52301

Marbleholics Anonymous
P.O. Box 251
Notus, ID 83656

Midwest Marble Club
Kenneth Royer, treasurer
3 Mallard Lane
St. Paul, MN 55127
Show, newsletter

Oklahoma Marble Collectors
c/o Neil or Debbie Thacker
16328 South Peoria
Bixby, OK 74008
Shows

Sea-Tac Marble Club
Larry Van Dyke
P.O. Box 336111
North Las Vegas, NV 89031
Shows, newsletter

South Jersey Marble Collectors
Joseph C. Brauner Jr.
7709 Raymond Drive
Millville, NJ 08322

Texas Marble Collectors
John W. Tays
417 Marsh Oval
New Braunfels, TX 78130
Shows, meeting

Tri-State Marble Collectors Club
David French
P.O. Box 18924
Fairfield, OH 45018
Show

Tulsa Area Marble Club
Cliff Mitchell
(918) 341-8310

West Virginia Marble Collectors Club
Paula Shepherd
Rt. 3 Box 91
Washington, WV 26181

Calendar of Meets: 2005

Date	Meet	Contact
January 13-15	**Crossroads of America Marble Show** Comfort Inn & Suites Indianapolis, IN (317) 875-7676	Beth or Greg Morris (765) 457-2477
February 12	**Buckeye Winterfest Marble Meet** Holiday Inn New Philadelphia, OH (330) 339-7731	Steve Smith (330) 364-8658
February 27	**Phoenix Marble Show** Four Points Sheraton Metro Center Phoenix, AZ (602) 997-5900	Bo Stiff (602) 298-0463
March 6	**KC "Marble Crazy" Show** Holiday Inn Overland Park, KS (913) 262-3010	Craig Snider (913) 268-9616
March 19	**Baltimore-Washington Marble Show** Perry Hall Middle School Perry Hall, MD	Jeanne Moss (410) 285-1829 Jen Pettie (410) 335-0404
March 19	**Ottawa Marble Show** Super 8 Motel Ottawa, IL (815) 434-2888	Daryl Anderson at the Super 8 Motel
April 2	**Sea-Tac Marble Collectors Show** Holiday Inn Seattle, WA (206) 248-1000	Larry Van Dyke (702) 656-1513
April 17	**Pride of the Prairie Show** Holiday Inn Select Decatur, IL (800) 408-7640	Denise Gregg (217) 795-4845 Chuck Garrett (217) 422-8454
April 23	**Texas Marble Collectors** Holiday Inn Arlington, TX (817) 640-7712	Calvin Griffith (817) 281-7755
April 30	**West Virginia Marble Festival** Comfort Suites Parkersburg, WV (304) 489-9500	Paula Shepherd (304) 863-5747
May 15	**Maine Marble Meet** Governor's Restaurant South Portland, ME (800) 528-1234	Mark Davis (207) 627-7318 Gary Stetson (207) 657-4165 Mickie Pasenen (207) 839-4726

Date	Meet	Contact
June 4-5	**Marble Collectors Unlimited** Holiday Inn-Amana Amana Colonies, IA (319) 668-1175	Gary Huxford (319) 642-3891
June 25-26	**Marble Artists and Collectors Conference** Wheaton Village Millville, NJ	Wheaton Village (800) 998-4552
June 25	**Tulsa Area Marble Collectors Show** Embassy Suites Tulsa, OK (800) Embassy	Cliff Mitchell (918) 341-9221 Don Bitzer (918) 254-4126
July 22-23	**Intl. Assoc. of Marble Collectors Show** South Center Best Western Tukwila, WA (800) 544-9863	Lee Linne (253) 815-6928 Ernie or Dani Kirk (253) 756-9771
August 6	**Buckeye Marble Collectors Meet** Radisson Hotel Worthington, OH (614) 436-0700	Liz Thompson (509) 783-3577 Brian Estepp (614) 863-5350
August 20	**Great Plains Marble Meet** Hampton Inn Council Bluffs, IA (712) 328-2500	Steve Campbell (712) 527-9162 Roy Katskee (402) 572-7512
September 10	**Crossroads of America Marble Show** Hampton Inn & Suites Kokomo, IN 46901 (765) 455-2900	Beth or Greg Morris (765) 457-2477
September 17	**Marble Meet** Holiday Inn Jonesboro Jonesboro, AR (870) 935-2030	Mark Carter (573) 695-3845 Sheila Ashabranner (870) 486-2218
September 24	**Sisterville Marble Show** The Wells Inn Sisterville, WV (304) 652-1312	Jim King (304) 652-4030
October __	**WV Marble Collectors Club** Amerihost Inn Parkersburg, WV (304) 424-5300	Ron and Paula Shepard (304) 863-5747
October 2	**Midwest Marble Club** Days Inn Airport/	Dale Fritz (651) 437-7383

	Mall of America Bloomington, MN 55425 (800) 558-5051	
October 8	**Pride of the Prairie Show** Country Inn & Suites Decatur, IL (217) 872-2402	Chuck Garrett (217) 422-8454 Guy or Denise Gregg (217) 795-4845
October 8-9	**Northeast Marble Meet** Radisson Inn Marlborough, MA (508) 480-0015	Bert Cohen (617) 247-4754
October 22	**Texas Marble Show** Holiday Inn New Braunfels, TX (830) 625-8017	Russ Behrndt (512) 388-9917
October 29	**Portland Marble Festival** Portland Waldorf School Milwaukie, OR	Chris Cooper (530) 459-1052
October 30	**Badger Marble Club Show** Holiday Inn East Madison, WI (608) 244-2481	Bill Bass (608) 723-6138 Art Jones (262) 673-5643
November 12	**Marble Collectors Show** Clarion-Emerald Springs Las Vegas, NV (800) 732-7889	Del Morgan (208) 453-1390 Lee Linne (253) 815-6928
December 4	**Tom and Huck Show** Clemens Hotel Hannibal, MO (800) 528-1234	John Hamon Miller (573) 221-3900 Jack Noonan (573) 221-4410